THE
GLUTEN-FREE FAMILY
COOKBOOK

This book is dedicated to you, the readers, and anyone and everyone who has struggled or still is struggling with food allergies.

Quarto.com

© 2023 Quarto Publishing Group USA Inc.
Text and Photographs © 2023 Lindsay Cotter

First Published in 2023 by Fair Winds Press, an imprint of The Quarto Group,
100 Cummings Center, Suite 265-D, Beverly, MA 01915, USA.
T (978) 282-9590 F (978) 283-2742

Fair Winds Press titles are also available at discount for retail, wholesale, promotional, and bulk purchase. For details, contact the Special Sales Manager by email at specialsales@quarto.com or by mail at The Quarto Group, Attn: Special Sales Manager, 100 Cummings Center, Suite 265-D, Beverly, MA 01915, USA.

27 26 25 24 23   2345

ISBN: 978-0-7603-8090-1
Digital edition published in 2023
eISBN: 978-0-7603-8091-8

Library of Congress Control Number: 2023930784

Design: Cindy Samargia Laun
Cover Image: Lindsay Cotter
Page Layout: Cindy Samargia Laun

Printed in USA

The information in this book is for educational purposes only. It is not intended to replace the advice of a physician or medical practitioner. Please see your health-care provider before beginning any new health program

THE
GLUTEN-FREE FAMILY
COOKBOOK

ALLERGY-FRIENDLY RECIPES
for Everyone Around Your Table

LINDSAY COTTER
Creator of Cotter Crunch

FAIR WINDS

CONTENTS

Introduction

Hello, there! I'm so happy you found this book!
I am Lindsay Cotter, and I'm a gluten-free nutrition specialist, and the founder of Cotter Crunch.

I'm also an imperfect human who is doing my best to fuel myself and my family with simple, allergy-friendly meals that are nourishing and delicious without breaking the bank!

It's likely that you deal with a number of food allergies and intolerances, or you know someone who does. If you feel overwhelmed and confused, trust me, I've been there. I know, firsthand, that navigating it all can be exhausting, and I'm here to help guide you through the journey. Consider me your cheerleader.

Every negative belief weakens the partnership between mind and body.

—DEEPAK CHOPRA

Food brings people together on many different levels. It's nourishment of the soul and body; it's truly love.

—GIADA DE LAURENTIIS

My Journey

Throughout the years, I have dealt with health conditions that have impacted my ability to consume, digest, and absorb a wide variety of foods. As a result, I was inspired to expand my degree in nutrition and bio-hacking obsessions beyond just fueling my professional triathlete husband, and I soon became an AASDN nutrition specialist.

Initially, my focus was purely sports performance nutrition, but over the years I turned my attention to overall wellness and gluten-free eating as I worked to heal myself from the inside out. Today, most of my symptoms remain dormant. The road to get here wasn't always easy, and I believe that it will never truly be "completed." After all, life is full of ups and downs, stress happens, and as much as we would like to be, no one is ever perfect.

This book began when I started to receive many last resort "cry for help" emails and messages from parents and individuals who were feeling overwhelmed and lost trying to navigate newly diagnosed food allergies and celiac disease in a food-centered world. As someone who has been (and sometimes still is) in that position, I know it's scary and you are looking for ways to make things better (and not worse).

With this book, I set out to create a resource and a message of hope. My goal is to reassure you that you can overcome the food obstacles you're facing while also truly enjoying mealtimes again. By learning the basics of nutrition and allergy-friendly cooking, you will be able to better understand your body and you can bounce back easily whenever setbacks do occur, without missing out on the foods and flavors you love!

With the utmost sincerity, I hope the recipes and information in this book can help calm the chaos of managing multiple food allergies—without breaking the bank or requiring hours in the kitchen. From the overwhelmed mom of four, to the newly single mother or father, recently diagnosed celiac, and everyone in between, I hope you find comfort in this book and that my recipes bring a sense of joy back into meals. I want you to have the tools to nourish yourself and your family with ease and bring everyone (food allergies or not) around the table with laughter and excitement again, and again, and again.

Speaking of gathering, there are many, many special people in my life who helped me research, write, and create this book. Please see acknowledgments and appreciations on page 170. Without them, all of this would not have been possible.

Food Philosophy

I'm a firm believer that at its core, food is meant to be used as fuel. By taking advantage of the natural vitamins, nutrients, and fiber found in wholesome ingredients, we can optimize, improve, and enhance our health. But its importance runs so much deeper than that. Like the Cotter pin, food is the single element that holds us all together. From family meals to birthday celebrations and holidays, it's at the center of all we do and it is meant to be enjoyed.

Yet, when food allergies and intolerances come into play, navigating food can be isolating, discouraging, and confusing. Options become limited, and what is available isn't always appealing or kid-friendly. As a result, it can become difficult to enjoy a single bite, let alone a complete meal—but it doesn't have to be that way!

This book brings you a host of recipes that are good for you, versatile, tasty, budget-friendly, and perfect for kids so you can bring the family around the table with their forks ready. You'll find lists of allergy-friendly pantry staples, cooking tips, and more to make homemade meals quick, easy, and enjoyable for everyone.

I focus on using natural ingredients in their simplest form to nourish and fuel the body from the inside out. No diet or way of living and eating is one size fits all: budgets, dietary needs, and preferences vary. So, please experiment with and customize each recipe to fit your specific needs. Don't stress over ingredients you don't have or foods your kids won't eat. Pick up and keep what works for you, and leave what doesn't. The rules are your own. Focus your energy on the recipes that bring you joy, and have fun creating meals that work for you and your family—whatever that looks like!

Common Food Allergies and Food Sensitivities

In my many years as a gluten-free nutrition specialist, I've found that allergies and intolerances are often confused and mistaken for each other. So, let's dive in and learn what they are, how to identify them, and the guidelines to follow to improve your health. After all, knowledge is power.

Food Allergies

Food allergies are immune system reactions that occur after eating a certain food. According to the United States Food and Drug Administration (FDA), the most common food allergies include milk, eggs, nuts, seeds, soy, wheat, fish, and shellfish. Contrary to popular belief, food allergy reactions do not always take place right away. In fact, there are two types of reactions that may occur. Anaphylaxis allergic reactions occur almost immediately and can be severe. The second type of reaction, known as non-IgE mediated food allergies, is much slower, taking up to several days to manifest, and is often less severe. Some people can have both reactions to one or multiple foods. So, it's important to look out for common symptoms such as those listed below.

Common Food Allergy Symptoms

The symptoms of food allergies can range from mild to severe. According to the Mayo Clinic, some of the most common reactions include but are not limited to:

- Skin irritations, such as hives or rash
- Swelling, especially around the face and tongue
- An itchy throat and/or difficulty swallowing
- Respiratory issues, such as coughing or shortness of breath
- Stomach distress, such as vomiting and/or diarrhea
- Feeling lightheaded or experiencing dizziness

Food Intolerances

Food intolerances are food sensitivities that occur when a person has difficulty digesting a certain food or displays a physical reaction, such as a skin rash, after consuming a food. According to the Cleveland Clinic, the most common food intolerances are lactose, histamine, and gluten. Each recipe in this book contains allergy-friendly ingredients, swaps, and substitutes to help meet all your needs!

Testing for Allergies & Intolerances

Not sure whether you have an allergy or an intolerance? You're not alone! The truth is, our digestive state is impacted by so much more than food, and intolerances can come and go. To help you get to the bottom of any digestive issues, go to https://www.ondemand.labcorp.com/lab-tests/food-allergy-test for information on testing.

Getting Started with a Gluten-Free and Allergy-Friendly Lifestyle

Whether you're new to gluten-free and allergy-friendly eating or you're a seasoned pro, I want to make it as stress free as possible. I feel the easiest way to do that is to get the whole family on board—but don't worry! You don't need to jump in all at once. Take what you need, and leave what you don't. Ready? You've got this. Deep breath. Let's dig in!

How to Plan Meals

In my opinion, planning ahead of time is key to creating stress-free meals the whole family can enjoy. For some, that means creating a meal plan for the whole week, but you can go as big or as small as you need! To start, I recommend having a rough plan for what you want to eat. Then, create a list of everything you'll need. This makes shopping and cooking a breeze, and it helps cut down on food waste.

Visit http://cottercrunch.com/grocerylist for a meal planner you can download for free!

Allergy-friendly eating doesn't have to cost an arm and a leg! By learning how to navigate the stores, you can feed your family for cheap!

Shop the perimeters. Fresh meat and produce are going to be more affordable than processed and packaged options.

Opt for seasonal ingredients. The fresher the food is, the more cost-effective it will be! If you can, stock up at your local farmers' market for vibrant fruit and vegetables.

Use frozen when you need to. Fruits and vegetables are picked and frozen at the peak of their ripeness, meaning they're oftentimes more nutrient-dense than their fresh counterparts.

Watch out for wholesale prices! While buying in bulk can be convenient for some items, sometimes it's actually more expensive. So, be sure to compare price tags before throwing items into your cart.

Check for certified gluten-free and allergy-friendly ingredients. Look out for brands that provide dedicated food labels and detailed nutrition information to ensure that your food is free from potential allergens, such as gluten or dairy.

Use subscriptions. There are tons of online options to get you what you need! Subscriptions such as Thrive Market can even help you find all your favorite products at a much cheaper rate.

Allergy-Friendly Appliances and How to Use Them

Air Fryer: Prepare small batches of all your favorite allergy-friendly foods without the need to dirty up extra baking sheets.

Slow Cooker: I love to use my slow cooker for soups, stews, dips, and comfort foods. Prepare recipes in the slow cooker. Then, for added flexibility, you can portion out a few servings before adding in extra ingredients that may not be so allergy-friendly.

Instant Pot: This is the perfect option to whip up pantry staples and make-ahead recipes. Dedicating a single Instant Pot to allergy-friendly foods (or meals) takes the stress out of meal prep.

Sheet Pans: Using color-coded sheet pans is the easiest way to keep meals and ingredients separate from one another.

Blenders: Blenders are a great tool to create gluten-free flours, smoothies, allergy-friendly bites, and more.

Color-Coded Food Storage Containers, Chopping Boards, and Knives: This is my biggest secret when it comes to stress-free cooking! Have dedicated storage containers, chopping boards, and utensils for specific foods, so that you always know what has been used. That way there's no risk of cross-contamination when it comes to food prep or storage.

Read the Labels

All ingredients included in packaged foods must be listed on the label. Look for labels such as "Certified Gluten-Free" and always double-check the ingredient list on the back of the package. If an ingredient is uncommon or unknown, it will still be listed as a common allergen like this: lecithin (soy) or flour (wheat). The FDA provides information on where to look for food allergens on food labels at https://www.fda.gov/food/food-labeling-nutrition/food-allergies.

Pantry, Fridge, and Freezer Staples

Once you've got a list of pantry staples, you'll have everything you need to make your own meals from scratch! With this list, you'll be able to create the base of all of the recipes in this book and branch out on your own with ease.

INGREDIENT	FLAVOR AND USES	FIND IT IN . . .
Veggie/Chicken Broth	Rich and savory. Use it to thin out soups, add depth to casseroles, reheat pastas and stir-fries, and add flavor to gluten-free grains.	Quick Southwestern Beef Soup (page 150) Nomato Sauce (page 38) Homemade Vegan Cheese Sauce (page 30)
Extra-Virgin Olive Oil	Slightly bitter and a little peppery. Has a high smoke point and is full of heart-healthy fats. Perfect for dressings, sautéing meat and veggies, and adding to soups.	Caesar Salad Jars with Crispy Chickpea "Croutons" (page 112)
Naturally Refined Avocado Oil	Fairly mild, slightly nutty. Use in many of the same ways as olive oil. Also great for baking due to mostly neutral flavor!	Basic Muffin Mix (page 50) Dairy-Free Sour Cream (page 36)
Naturally Refined Coconut Oil	Neutral in flavor. Rich in medium-chain fatty acids. Can be used in most recipes to replace other oils or even butter.	Allergy-Friendly Cupcakes (page 162)
Toasted Sesame Oil	Nutty. A little goes a long way! Great for adding a boost of flavor to dressings, marinades, sauces, soups, and stews.	Soy-Free Stir-Fry Sauce (page 40)
Apple Cider Vinegar	Tart. Can be combined with nondairy milk to make a buttermilk substitute for recipes. Also great added to marinades, salads, and veggies.	Plant-Powered Protein Pancakes (page 60) Egg-Free Mayo (page 41) Microwave English Muffins (page 88)
Coconut Aminos	Gluten-free soy sauce alternative. Salty with a hint of sweetness. Great for stir-fries, soups, and sauces.	Soy-Free Stir-Fry Sauce (page 40)
Spices: Kosher/Sea Salt, Ground Black Pepper, Cumin, Paprika, Italian Blend, Cayenne, Chili Powder, Garlic Powder, Etc.	Use to add robust flavor to any dish. Can provide a good source of antioxidants and anti-inflammatory properties! Use in everything from baked goods to salad dressings and casseroles.	"Cheesy" Tomato Soup with Crispy Chickpeas (page 104) Tuna Patties (page 126)
Fresh and Dried Herbs: Oregano, Rosemary, Parsley, Mint, Basil, Etc.	Used to add flavor to any dish. They're also a great source of vitamins and antioxidants.	Baked Italian Turkey Meatballs (page 128) Nomato Sauce (page 38)
Garlic	Pungent, zesty when raw. Use cooked to add a buttery sweetness to stir-fries, casseroles, and sheet-pan meals.	Creamy Roasted Cauliflower Toscana (page 148) Green Bean Chicken Casserole (page 142)
Onion	Use raw to add a spicy zest to salads. Use the sweeter, umami flavor of cooked onions in soups, stews, casseroles, skillet recipes, and sheet-pan meals.	Sheet-Pan BBQ Peach Salmon and Vegetables (page 119) Asian Noodle Jars (page 111)
Lemons and Limes	Refreshing and citrusy. Use to cut through the fat in dishes and provide a light flavor.	Quick Southwestern Beef Soup (page 150) Chicken Salad Two Ways (page 98) Honey Mustard Dressing (page 47)

INGREDIENT	FLAVOR AND USES	FIND IT IN . . .
Frozen Produce: Green Beans, Berries, Peas, Carrots, Etc.	Add a savory or sweet element, plus vitamins, nutrients, and fiber. Use fruit in smoothies, desserts, salads, yogurt bowls, and oatmeal. Use veggies in salads, casseroles, sheet-pan meals, skillet recipes, smoothies, soups, and anything else you can think of!	Smoothies (page 69–77) Hidden Veggie Mac and Cheese (page 138) Green Bean Chicken Casserole (page 142)
Sweet Potatoes/Yams	Sweet and starchy, with an immense amount of vitamin C, potassium, and fiber. Use in savory breakfast hashes and casseroles or sweet side dishes.	Mexican Sweet Potato Patties (page 96) Sweet Potato "No Peanut" Stew (page 152)
BPA-Free Canned Tomatoes	Slightly sweet and a little tart. Full of vitamin C. Use for the base of soups, stews, and sauces. Or add them to salads and cooked dishes.	"Cheesy" Tomato Soup with Crispy Chickpeas (page 104) Mexican Rice Casserole (page 141)
Certified Gluten-Free Rolled Oats	Neutral-tasting complex starch; high in fiber, vitamins, and nutrients; higher in protein than other grains. Make oatmeal and no-bake cookies, or grind into a flour for gluten-free muffins and cakes.	No-Bake Apple Cinnamon Energy Bites (page 82) Mexican Sweet Potato Patties (page 96) Chicken and Waffles (page 124)
Starches: Arrowroot, Tapioca, Non-GMO Cornstarch	Use to thicken soups, stews, baked goods, and casseroles.	Creamy Dairy-Free Mushroom Soup (page 146) Sheet-Pan Coconut Crust Chicken (page 118)
Nutritional Yeast	Excellent source of B vitamins and plant-based protein. Use as a thickener in soups and sauces. Can also add a cheesy flavor in vegan dishes.	Homemade Vegan Cheese Sauce (page 30) "Cheesy" Tomato Soup with Crispy Chickpeas (page 104)
Quinoa	Fairly neutral in taste. Use as a high-protein replacement for rice. Add to soups, stews, bowls, and casseroles.	Mezza Power Lunch Bowl (page 114)
Rice	Naturally gluten-free. Takes on the flavor of whatever it is paired with. Use as a base for bowls and casseroles, add it to salads and soups, or sweeten it for a dessert.	Mexican Rice Casserole (page 141)
Nondairy Milk: Oat Milk, Soymilk, Coconut Milk, Cashew Milk, and Hemp Milk	All are fairly mild and just a little bit sweet. Use them for drinking, smoothies, ice cream, desserts, cereal, sauces, and soups.	Smoothies (pages 69–77) Plant-Powered Protein Pancakes (page 60) Customizable Chia Pudding Cups (page 56)
Nuts and Seeds: Sunflower, Pumpkin, and Cashews	Used to achieve a creamy, dairy, or cheese-like texture and taste in casseroles, sauces, and dips.	Dairy-Free Sour Cream (page 36) Cheesy Seedy Crackers (page 86) Almond Flour (page 25)
Flaxseed/Chia Seed	Use to thicken smoothies or soups, and as a boost of plant-based protein and healthy fats. Use in vegan baking to replace eggs.	No-Bake Apple Cinnamon Energy Bites (page 82) Flax egg in Tuna Patties (page 126)

Bonus! Nutrition and Baking Boosters

INGREDIENT	FLAVOR AND USES	FIND IT IN . . .
Plant-Based Protein Powder	A good source of high-quality protein used to boost the nutritional value, flavor, and texture of many recipes.	Protein Power Smoothie (page 71) Chocolate Protein Muffins (page 52)
Collagen Peptides— Grass-Fed Beef or Marine	A protein source naturally found in the body. Helps improve the consistency of recipes. The boost of protein can help improve hair, skin, joints, and nails.	Chocolate Protein Muffins (page 52) Smoothies (pages 69–77)
Grass-Fed Beef Gelatin	Good source of protein. Used in gummies and Jell-O, and to thicken soups and smoothies. Can help improve gut health and joint health.	Collagen Fruit Gummies (page 87)
Unsweetened Coconut Flakes	Excellent source of healthy fats and fiber. Use in recipes and as a garnish for a light fruity taste and extra chewy texture.	Chocolate Coconut Protein Balls (page 83) Sheet-Pan Coconut Crust Chicken (page 118)

Allergy-Friendly Swaps and Substitutions

Allergy-friendly eating doesn't mean you have to give up all your favorite foods and recipes! Keep this chart on hand for easy swaps and substitutes to replicate your favorite flavors with ease. *Note: The FDA lists coconut as a tree nut though many experts disagree with this. Coconut is a seed of a drupaceous fruit. The majority of people allergic to tree nuts can safely eat coconut. That being said, it's best to talk to your allergist about adding or removing coconut to your diet if you have a nut allergy.*

NEED TO SUBSTITUTE	CONSIDER THESE	YOU CAN MAKE THESE! HERE'S HOW
Egg (for baking)	Flax egg Grass-fed gelatin Arrowroot/tapioca starch Canned chickpeas and brine	n/a
Mayonnaise	No-egg mayo (store-bought or homemade using chickpea brine)	Egg-Free Mayo (page 41)
Cow milk	Oat milk Coconut milk Seed milk (Ex. hemp milk)	Gluten-Free Oat Milk (page 28) Hemp Seed Milk (page 26)
Cheese	Vegan cheese plus cheese sauce recipes Nutritional yeast (make sure it's certified gluten-free)	Homemade Vegan Cheese Sauce (page 30)
Whipped cream	Coconut whip	Coconut Cream Frosting/ Whipped Cream (page 32)
Frosting	Coconut whip	Coconut Cream Frosting/ Whipped Cream (page 32)
Sour cream	Vegan sour cream (store-bought or homemade dairy-free sour cream)	Dairy-Free Sour Cream (page 36)
Peanut butter	Almond butter Cashew butter Sunflower seed butter	Sunflower Seed Butter (page 42)

Egg   Dairy   Peanut   Wheat   Soy   Nightshades

NEED TO SUBSTITUTE	CONSIDER THESE	YOU CAN MAKE THESE! HERE'S HOW
Whole-grain wheat	Amaranth Buckwheat Millet Certified gluten-free oats Quinoa Rice	n/a
Wheat/white flour	Gluten-free oat flour Homemade millet flour Almond flour Cassava flour Coconut flour Rice flour Tapioca flour Potato starch	Millet Flour (page 24) Oat Flour (page 22) Almond Flour (page 25)
Wheat pasta	Black bean pasta Chickpeas Chickpea pasta Lentil pasta Potato pasta or gluten-free gnocchi Quinoa pasta	n/a
Wheat-based thickener	Arrowroot powder Cornstarch (non-GMO) Rice flour Gluten-free oat flour	Oat Flour (page 22)
Soy sauce	Coconut aminos	No-Soy Stir-Fry Sauce (page 40)
Stir-fry sauce	No-Soy Stir-Fry Sauce recipe	No-Soy Stir-Fry Sauce (page 40)
Soybean oil	Olive oil (extra-virgin and light) Avocado oil (naturally refined) Coconut oil (naturally refined and extra virgin)	n/a
Tomato sauce	Nomato Sauce	Nomato Sauce (page 38)

Sample Allergy-Friendly Meal Plans

Allergies and intolerances don't have to put a burden on meal planning. Whether you're preparing meals for yourself or a loved one, use these sample meal plans to make dairy-free, nut-free, or grain-free planning a little easier. *Note: Every meal is also gluten-free!*

Egg-Free Meal Plan

BREAKFAST	LUNCH	DINNER	SNACK
Breakfast Sausage Bites (page 62) or Protein Power Smoothie (page 71)	Mezza Power Lunch Bowl (page 114) or Chicken Salad Two Ways (page 98)	Sheet-Pan Cauliflower Tacos (page 120) or Green Bean Chicken Casserole (page 142)	Chocolate Coconut Protein Balls (page 83)

Dairy-Free Meal Plan

BREAKFAST	LUNCH	DINNER	SNACK
Plant-Powered Protein Pancakes (page 60) or Blueberry Oat Muffins (pages 50–51)	Mexican Sweet Potato Patties (page 96) and/or "Cheesy" Tomato Soup with Crispy Chickpeas (page 104)	Sheet-Pan Coconut Crust Chicken (page 118)	Cheesy Seedy Crackers (page 86) and Collagen Fruit Gummies (page 87)

Nut-Free Meal Plan

BREAKFAST	LUNCH	DINNER	SNACK
Customizable Chia Pudding Cups (page 56)	Salmon Salad Stuffed Mini Bell Peppers (page 106) or Creamy Tuscan Pasta Salad (page 108)	Sheet-Pan BBQ Peach Salmon and Vegetables (page 119)	Hidden Veggie Smoothie (page 70)

Egg   Dairy   Peanut   Wheat   Soy   Nightshades

1 DIY Pantry and Fridge Staples

This chapter is your go-to guide for all things sauces, condiments, and swaps. You'll find homemade gluten-free flours, dairy-free substitutes, and more to stock your pantry and fridge with wholesome options the whole family will love. Simple to make, with no mess and no fuss, these recipes are incorporated throughout the book, and they can also be used on their own to add texture and flavor to your favorite meals.

OAT FLOUR

Gluten-free | Dairy-free | Vegetarian | Vegan | Nut-free | Egg-free

Prep Time | 5 minutes

Makes | About 2 cups (192–200 g)

Oat flour is a whole-grain, gluten-free flour alternative made from ground whole oats. It's budget-friendly and quick to make. The texture is tender and it has a slightly nutty taste, making it perfect for pancakes, biscuits, and cookies.

2 cups (192–200g) gluten-free old-fashioned rolled, quick-cooking, or steel-cut oats

1. Place half the oats in a high-speed blender or food processor. Blend or pulse for 45 seconds, or until a fine, flour-like consistency is formed. Scrape the sides of the blender/food processor, and blend again for up to 2 minutes, or until a fine flour is formed.
2. Transfer the ground oats to an airtight container. Repeat with the remaining oats.

Notes
- Steel-cut oats may take longer to blend.
- Whole-grain gluten-free flours contain natural oils, meaning that their shelf life is not as long as that of refined flours.
- The volume of oat flour can vary due to the milling process. I recommend weighing the flour for all recipes to ensure proper amounts.

Storage
- Store in an airtight container at room temperature for 2 to 3 months, or in the freezer for up to 6 months.

MILLET FLOUR

Gluten-free | Dairy-free | Vegetarian |
Vegan | Nut-free | Egg-free

Prep Time | 5 minutes

Makes | 1½–2 cups (360 g)

Millet flour is a gluten-free baking essential, and it's one of our favorites! Lighter, softer, and silkier than other gluten-free flours, it has a subtle creamy flavor perfect for baked goods, such as biscuits, pancakes, and bread!

2 cups (360 g) hulled millet

1. Place half the hulled millet in a high-speed blender or food processor. Blend or pulse for 45 seconds, or until a fine flour-like consistency is formed.
2. Transfer the ground millet to an airtight container. Repeat with the remaining hulled millet.

Note
- I recommend weighing the flour for all recipes to ensure proper amounts.

Storage
- Store in an airtight container at room temperature for 2 to 3 months, in the fridge for up to 6 months, or freeze for up to 1 year.

ALMOND FLOUR

Gluten-free | Dairy-free | Vegetarian | Vegan | Egg-free

Prep Time | 5 minutes

Makes | 1½ cups (175 g)

A staple gluten-free flour, almond flour is made from blanched peeled almonds. It has a fine texture and nutty flavor. The higher fat content makes it perfect for pairing with oat and/or millet flour for soft baked goods.

1½–1⅔ cups (166–184 g) slivered blanched almonds

1. Place the almonds in a high-speed blender or food processor. Blend/pulse on high speed for 5 to 10 seconds, or until a fine meal is formed. Do not over blend. If clumps or large pieces of almonds remain, scrape the sides with a spatula, and pulse again.
2. Transfer the almond flour to an airtight container.

Note
- Use in any recipe that calls for almond flour or almond meal. Do not use almond flour as a 1:1 substitute for gluten-free flour blends. I recommend weighing the flour for all recipes to ensure proper amounts.

Storage
- Store in an airtight container at room temperature for 2 to 3 months, or freeze for up to 6 months.

HEMP SEED MILK

Gluten-free | Dairy-free | Vegetarian | Vegan | Nut-free | Egg-free

Prep Time | 12 hours 15 minutes

Makes | 4 servings

Hemp milk is a rich and creamy dairy-free milk alternative for those who cannot tolerate nut milk. It has a mild, earthy taste, and it's great for hot or cold cereal, smoothies, and baked goods.

½ cup (80 g) hulled hemp seed or hemp seed hearts

3 cups (705 ml) purified water

Pinch of sea salt

1 teaspoon pure vanilla extract (optional)

¼ cup (60 g) sweetener, such as honey, maple syrup, or monk fruit (optional)

MIX-INS (OPTIONAL)

½ frozen banana, sliced

1 tablespoon (5 g) unsweetened cocoa powder

⅓ cup (50 g) fresh berries

2 tablespoons (28 g) chopped coconut butter or nut butter (to make extra creamy)

1. Add all the ingredients to a high-speed blender. Blend for 2 minutes, or until smooth. The hemp seeds should blend into the milk. For an extra smooth texture, remove any excess seeds by pouring the milk through a layer of cheesecloth, a nut milk bag, or a fine-mesh strainer.
2. Add mix-ins (if using) to the blender. Add the strained milk back to the blender and blend until creamy. For fruit-flavored mix-ins, strain again to remove any seeds or flesh.
3. Pour the milk into an airtight container. Cover and chill for 6 to 12 hours.

Note
- For a creamier consistency, use 1 part hemp seeds to 3 parts water.

Storage
- Store in an airtight container in the fridge for up to 5 days.

GLUTEN-FREE OAT MILK

Gluten-free | Dairy-free | Vegetarian |
Vegan | Nut-free | Egg-free

Prep Time | 5 minutes

Makes | 5 servings

Over the last few years, oat milk has exploded in popularity, and it's no secret why! A longtime favorite of mine, it's made by extracting liquid from whole-grain, gluten-free oats, which results in a mild sweet flavor you'll love.

1 cup (96 g) gluten-free, old-fashioned rolled oats

4–5 cups (940–1200 ml) purified water, cold

2 tablespoons (30 ml) maple syrup or 3 pitted dates (optional)

Pinch of kosher salt

MIX-INS (OPTIONAL)

1 frozen banana, sliced

1 tablespoon (5 g) unsweetened cocoa powder

⅓ cup (50 g) fresh berries

2 tablespoons (28 g) chopped coconut butter or Sunflower Seed Butter (page 42, to make extra creamy)

PROTEIN BOOSTER (OPTIONAL)

2–3 scoops (16–25 g) any flavor collagen or plant-based collagen

1. Place the oats and 4 cups (940 ml) of water in a blender. Blend on high speed for 30 seconds, or until they are broken down into a very fine meal. Do not over blend; blending too long will warm the oats, creating a slimy texture.
2. Add more water if you prefer a thinner milk. Add syrup (if using) and salt, and blend again.
3. Strain the milk through a layered cheesecloth or a fine-mesh bag in a colander over a large bowl. Let the liquid drip through. Do not squeeze the excess oat pulp through the strainer! This will create a gummy texture.
4. Add mix-ins (if using) to the blender. Add the strained milk and blend until creamy. For fruit-flavored mix-ins, strain once more to remove any seeds or flesh. Whisk or blend in the collagen (if using).
5. Pour the milk into an airtight container. Cover and chill for 6 to 12 hours.

Notes
- Oat milk may form a small layer of film or separation at the top. This is natural. Shake the oat milk before serving.
- See page 167 for collagen suggestions.

Storage
- Store in an airtight container in the fridge for up to 5 days.

HOMEMADE VEGAN CHEESE SAUCE

Gluten-free | Dairy-free | Vegetarian | Vegan | Nut-free

Prep Time | 5 minutes

Cook Time | 5 minutes

Makes | 1 cup (235 ml)

This is the only vegan cheese sauce you'll ever need. It is so creamy and full of flavor, you'll never guess that it's dairy-free and good for you, too! Use it in soups, stews, casseroles, and everything in between.

1¼ cups (295 ml) canned full-fat coconut milk

¼ cup (60 ml) vegetable broth

⅔ cup (40–50 g) nutritional yeast

1 tablespoon (15 ml) lemon juice

1 teaspoon garlic powder

1 teaspoon onion powder

1 tablespoon (9 g) arrowroot starch or cornstarch

½ teaspoon kosher salt

½ teaspoon smoked paprika

¾ cup (90 g) diced and steamed carrot (1 large)

MIX-INS (OPTIONAL)

¼–⅓ cup (40–55 g) canned green chiles or jalapeño

1. In a medium saucepan over medium heat, whisk all the ingredients except the carrots and chiles (if using).
2. Simmer for 5 minutes, stirring occasionally. Carefully pour into a high-speed blender and add the carrots. Alternatively, use an immersion blender to blend the ingredients in the saucepan. Blend for 1 to 2 minutes, or until completely smooth. For a spicier version, mix in the chiles.

Notes

- For a tangier cheese sauce, add a splash of apple cider vinegar or gluten-free Worcestershire sauce.
- Serve immediately or store the sauce in the fridge for up to 4 days. The texture will change and thicken once chilled. To thin it out, reheat it in a saucepan and whisk in 1 to 2 tablespoons (15 to 30 ml) nondairy milk or broth if needed.

Storage

- Store in an airtight container in the fridge for up to 5 days.

COCONUT CREAM FROSTING/WHIPPED CREAM

Gluten-free | Grain-free | Dairy-free |
Vegetarian | Vegan | Nut-free | Egg-free

Prep Time | 24 hours

Makes | 1¼–1½ cups (250–300 g)

This is my go-to dairy-free alternative to traditional whipped cream. It looks and tastes extravagant, but it is easy to make. Don't worry if you're not a fan of coconut! It just adds a little sweetness for the perfect flavor.

2 cans (13.6 ounces, or 386 ml, each) coconut cream

¼–⅓ cup (60–80 ml) maple syrup or ⅓–½ cup (40–60 g) confectioners' sugar (to taste)

1 teaspoon pure vanilla extract

1–2 tablespoons (9–18 g) arrowroot starch (if needed)

CHOCOLATE OPTION

¼ cup (20 g) Dutch process cocoa powder

1. Place the coconut cream cans in the fridge for 12 to 24 hours to harden. Remove the canned coconut cream from the fridge, being careful not to shake the can. Remove the thickened coconut cream (top portion) and place into a stand mixer bowl or mixing bowl. Discard the coconut water portion or save for another use.
2. Add the sweetener of choice and vanilla. Whip in the stand mixer or with a handheld mixer on high speed until the cream is light and fluffy.
3. If making chocolate frosting, add the cocoa powder and whip again until combined and fluffy.
4. If the frosting isn't firming up, add the arrowroot starch and whip to the desired thickness.

Note
- Coconut cream softens in the heat, so be sure to frost cakes and cupcakes quickly, then place in the fridge to set. Frosted cakes/cupcakes will hold at room temperature for 2 to 3 hours depending on the environment.

Storage
- Store in an airtight container in the fridge for 4 to 5 days.

2 } Sauce Swaps and Condiments

Nobody likes bland food, but the sauces and condiments found in the store are often loaded with allergens and strange ingredients. Or they cost an arm and a leg. So, I decided to do something about it! In this chapter, you'll find my go-to sauces and condiments for salads, marinades, dipping, and more. Each recipe is used throughout the book, and they can easily be added to the meals you already make and love.

DAIRY-FREE SOUR CREAM

Gluten-free | Dairy-free | Vegetarian | Vegan | Nut-free Option | Egg-free

Prep Time | 5 minutes

Cook Time | 20 minutes

Makes | 1½ cups (360 g)

This vegan version is creamy, rich, and tangy just like regular sour cream. It is good for your gut too, thanks to the use of probiotics. Smear it on gluten-free sandwiches, and mix it in casseroles. Add it to baked goods and more.

1 cup (145 g) raw sunflower seeds or raw cashews

1 cup (235 ml) purified water

¼ cup (60 ml) lemon juice

1 teaspoon sea salt

1–2 teaspoons (5–10 ml) distilled white vinegar or apple cider vinegar

1 teaspoon Dijon mustard

1–2 teaspoons (8–15 g) tapioca starch or cornstarch

Powder from 1 probiotic capsule (optional)

MIX-INS (OPTIONAL)

2 teaspoons (1 g) dried chives or ¼ cup (12 g) chopped fresh chives

1 teaspoon garlic powder

½ teaspoon onion powder

1. Add the seeds or cashews to a large bowl. Add enough boiling water to cover. Soak for 20 minutes to soften. Drain the seeds/nuts and discard the water.
2. Place the seeds/nuts in a high-speed blender and add the purified water, lemon juice, sea salt, vinegar, Dijon mustard, and tapioca starch. Pulse until creamy, no longer than 5 minutes.
3. Add the probiotic powder and mix-ins (if using). Store in the fridge in an airtight container.

Notes
- Cashews have a neutral flavor. Sunflower seeds have more of a seed-like aftertaste; you may need mix-ins to reach the best flavor.
- For a creamier sauce, swap out the 1 cup (235 ml) purified water for ½ cup (120 ml) canned coconut cream and ½ cup (120 ml) purified water.
- The probiotic powder helps give that cultured taste similar to classic sour cream as it stores in the fridge.

Storage
- Store in an airtight container in the fridge for up to 2 weeks.

NOMATO SAUCE

Gluten-free | Grain-free | Dairy-free |
Vegetarian | Vegan | Nut-free | Egg-free

Prep Time | 10 minutes

Cook Time | 10 minutes

Makes | 2¾ cups (645 ml)

A play on words, nomato sauce is my take on an allergy-friendly, nightshade-free tomato sauce that features a whole host of hidden veggies. Now you can have your pasta, and eat it, too!

1 tablespoon (15 ml) olive oil

⅔ cup (110 g) chopped yellow onion

2 cloves garlic, minced, or
1 teaspoon garlic powder

1 cup (136 g) diced beets
(1 large raw beet)

1 cup (130 g) diced carrots
(1–2 large carrots, peeled)

1 teaspoon dried Italian seasoning

1 teaspoon dried oregano

¼ teaspoon kosher salt

1½ cups (355 ml) vegetable broth,
divided, plus more to taste

1 cup (244 g) canned or fresh pumpkin
or squash purée

1 tablespoon (4 g) chopped fresh parsley

1 tablespoon (15 ml) lemon juice and/or
2 teaspoons (10 ml) balsamic vinegar

ADD-INS (OPTIONAL)

1 tablespoon (8 g) pitted diced olives

1 tablespoon (9 g) capers, drained

1 tablespoon (5 g) nutritional yeast

1. In a large skillet over medium heat, heat the oil. Add the onions and cook until tender and caramelized, 7 to 10 minutes. Add the garlic and cook for 1 minute, or until fragrant. Add the beets, carrots, Italian seasoning, oregano, and salt. Stir to combine.
2. Add 1 cup (235 ml) of the broth. Cover and cook for 20 to 30 minutes, or until the carrots and beets are fork tender. The broth should be fully absorbed.
3. Transfer the ingredients to a high-speed blender. Add the remaining ½ cup (120 ml) broth and the pumpkin purée. Blend until smooth. Add more broth until the desired consistency is reached.
4. Add the parsley, lemon juice and/or vinegar, and add-ins (if using). Blend until smooth. Transfer the sauce back to the skillet and simmer over medium heat for 10 minutes.

Note
- For a sweeter sauce, use purple beets. For a lighter, more neutral flavor, use golden beets.

Storage
- Store in an airtight container in the fridge for up to 1 week, or store cooled sauce in the freezer for up to 1 month.

SOY-FREE STIR-FRY SAUCE

Gluten-free | Dairy-free | Vegetarian |
Nut-free | Egg-free

Prep Time | 2 minutes

Makes | 1½ cups (355 ml)

My secret weapon for no-fuss weeknight meals, this sauce is the perfect balance of savory and sweet. Just add water and it's good to go for fish, veggies, and chicken!

BASE

⅓ cup (80 ml) coconut aminos or gluten-free Worcestershire sauce

2 tablespoons (30 ml) dry sherry

¼ cup (60 ml) gluten-free oyster sauce or vegetable broth

1 tablespoon (20 g) honey (optional)

1 tablespoon (15 ml) toasted sesame oil

2 tablespoons (18 g) arrowroot or cornstarch

Lemon juice or rice vinegar

ADD-INS

2 teaspoons (4 g) grated fresh ginger

2 teaspoons (6 g) minced garlic

1 teaspoon red pepper flakes

1. Add all the ingredients to a jar with a lid. Shake to combine.

Note
- See page 167 for gluten-free Worcestershire sauce suggestions.

Storage
- Store in an airtight container in the fridge for up to 3 weeks. Shake before each use.

EGG-FREE MAYO

Gluten-free | Grain-free | Dairy-free |
Vegetarian | Vegan | Nut-free | Egg-free

Prep Time | 10 minutes

Makes | 1 cup (225 g)

I keep a big jar of this mayo in my fridge at all times. Unlike other varieties made with mystery ingredients, this comes together with just a few whole-food staples you can feel good about eating. Use it for sandwiches, pasta salads, casseroles, and more.

¼ cup (60 ml) chickpea brine

¼ teaspoon garlic powder (optional)

1–2 teaspoons (5–10 ml) distilled white vinegar

Kosher salt

1 teaspoon Dijon mustard or ½ teaspoon dry mustard powder

¾–1 cup (177–235 ml) naturally refined avocado oil

1. In a mixing bowl, add the chickpea brine, garlic powder (if using), vinegar, salt to taste, and mustard. Whip the ingredients together using an electric beater for 1 to 2 minutes, until the mixture begins to increase in volume. It should look like egg white foam.
2. Pour into a tall airtight container. Using an immersion blender or hand blender on high speed, slowly stream in the oil until the mixture thickens (emulsifies), 1 to 2 minutes. Start with ¾ cup (180 ml) and add more to your preference; the more oil that is used, the creamier, thicker, and denser the texture will become. Chill in the fridge before using.

Notes
- Chickpea brine is the leftover liquid from canned chickpeas.
- Do not use a wide-rimmed food processor, and be sure to follow the steps exactly. Any alterations could result in an oily dressing instead of a smooth emulsion.

Storage
- Store in an airtight container in the fridge for up to 2 weeks.

SUNFLOWER SEED BUTTER

Gluten-free | Grain-free | Dairy-free | Vegetarian | Vegan | Nut-free | Egg-free

Prep Time | 5 minutes

Cook Time | 20 minutes

Makes | 1½ cups (390 g)

If you've never had sunflower seed butter, prepare for your world to be changed! It's smooth, earthy, and so tasty you'll want to eat it by the spoonful. It's also great in energy bites and oatmeal.

3 cups (435 g) raw sunflower seeds

2 teaspoons (5 g) ground cinnamon

Pinch of kosher salt

2–3 teaspoons (10–15 ml) melted naturally refined coconut oil or avocado oil, as needed

ADD-INS (OPTIONAL)

1 teaspoon pure vanilla extract

2–4 tablespoons (40–80 g) honey or maple syrup, to taste

1. Preheat the oven to 350°F (175°C).
2. In a large bowl, place the sunflower seeds, cinnamon, and salt and toss to evenly coat. Spread evenly on a sheet pan. Bake for 15 to 20 minutes, or until golden brown, stirring the seeds halfway through to toast evenly.
3. Place the toasted sunflower seeds in the bowl of a food processor. Blend on high speed for 1 to 2 minutes, or until a mealy texture is formed. Scrape down the sides of the bowl. Continue blending on medium to high speed for 7 to 10 minutes, or until a thick paste is formed.
4. Add the add-ins (if using), and blend to combine. Add the oil as needed until the desired consistency is reached.

Storage
- Store in an airtight container at room temperature for up to 1 week, or in the fridge for up to 1 month.

ALLERGY-FRIENDLY CAESAR DRESSING

Gluten-free | Grain-free | Dairy-free
Option | Vegetarian | Nut-free | Egg-free

Prep Time | 10 minutes

Makes | About 1 cup (235 ml)

Perfect for dipping, dunking, and drizzling, this Caesar dressing is bursting with flavor. And it's so creamy you'd never guess that it's egg-free, nut-free, and gluten-free! There's a dairy-free option, too!

2 tablespoons (30 g) plain hummus or 1 tablespoon (14 g) Egg-Free Mayo (page 41)

2 tablespoons (30 ml) lemon juice

2 tablespoons (30 g) Dijon mustard

1½–2 teaspoons (7–10 ml) gluten-free Worcestershire sauce

1 large clove garlic or 2 teaspoons (6 g) minced garlic

½ cup (120 ml) extra-virgin olive oil, plus more if needed

½ cup (50 g) grated Parmesan cheese, hemp seeds, or nutritional yeast

½ teaspoon kosher salt

Black pepper

Onion or garlic powder (if using hemp seeds; optional)

1. In a small bowl, combine the hummus, lemon juice, Dijon mustard, Worcestershire sauce, and garlic. Slowly drizzle in the olive oil, whisking continuously. For a thinner dressing, add an extra 1 to 2 tablespoons (15 to 30 ml) of olive oil.
2. Whisk in the Parmesan cheese, salt, and pepper. If using hemp seeds, it's best to use a blender to combine for a smoother texture. Transfer to an airtight container and chill in the fridge.

Notes
- For a dairy-free option, omit the Parmesan cheese and use nutritional yeast or hemp seeds, adding onion or garlic powder if desired.
- See page 167 for gluten-free Worcestershire sauce suggestions.

Storage
- Store in an airtight container in the fridge for up to 1 week.

AVOCADO RANCH

Gluten-free | Grain-free | Dairy-free |
Vegetarian | Vegan | Nut-free

Prep Time | 5 minutes

Makes | About 1 cup (235 ml)

This recipe is just like store-bought ranch but better. It has a boost of healthy fats and flavor thanks to the avocado. Spread it on sandwiches or use it as a dip. Try it in the Avocado Ranch Turkey Roll-Ups (page 102) and Salmon Salad Stuffed Mini Bell Peppers (page 106).

VEGAN BUTTERMILK

⅓ cup (80 ml) unsweetened nondairy milk (higher fat content is best)

1 teaspoon vinegar or lemon juice

AVOCADO RANCH

⅔ cup (100 g) diced avocado
(about 1 medium ripe avocado)

⅔–¾ cup (160–180 ml) neutral oil such as olive or naturally refined avocado oil

⅓ cup (80 ml) vegan buttermilk

1 tablespoon (3 g) minced fresh chives or 1 tablespoon (1 g) dried chives

1 tablespoon (1 g) chopped fresh cilantro

2 teaspoons (10 ml) apple cider vinegar or lime/lemon juice

1 teaspoon garlic powder

½ teaspoon onion powder

1 teaspoon ground cumin

Kosher salt and black pepper

1. To make the vegan buttermilk: In a bowl, combine the milk and lemon juice or vinegar. Let sit at room temperature for 5 minutes to curdle.
2. To make the avocado ranch: Add the buttermilk and avocado ranch ingredients to a food processor or high-speed blender. Pulse to combine. Adjust the seasonings, if desired.
3. Pour into an airtight container and refrigerate 2 to 3 hours before serving.

Note
- For a thinner dressing, blend in 1 to 3 tablespoons (15 to 45 ml) more oil or water.

Storage
- Store in an airtight container in the fridge for up to 1 week.

HONEY MUSTARD DRESSING

Gluten-free | Grain-free | Dairy-free |
Vegetarian | Nut-free | Egg-free

Prep Time | 5 minutes

Makes | ⅔ cup (160 ml)

A little sweet, a little spicy, and a lot delicious, this dressing is great to have on hand to use on salads and as a dip for veggies.

¼ cup (60 g) Dijon mustard

3–4 tablespoons (60–80 g) honey, or to taste

1 teaspoon onion powder

¼–½ teaspoon sweet paprika or smoked paprika (optional)

1 teaspoon lemon juice

¼ cup (60 ml) extra-virgin olive oil, plus more if needed

Kosher salt and black pepper

⅓–½ cup (75–112 g) Egg-Free Mayo (page 41) or plain yogurt (optional)

1. In a small mixing bowl, add the Dijon, honey, onion powder, paprika (if using), lemon juice, and oil. Whisk until smooth. Alternatively, add all of the ingredients to the bowl of a food processor. Process on high speed until creamy and smooth. Season with salt and pepper.

Note
- Add more oil for a thinner dressing, or add the mayo or yogurt for a creamier dressing.

Storage
- Store in an airtight container for up to 7 days.

3 { Breakfast

Mornings can go by in a rush, but that doesn't mean you have to walk out the door hungry! In this chapter, you'll find everything from bars and bites to muffins, sausage, and more. These recipes are easy to make ahead of time, so you can grab them as you're running out the door. Or pick your favorite weekend brunch for a sit-down meal that will have the whole family excited to wake up.

Blueberry Oat Muffins, pages 50–51

BASIC MUFFIN MIX

Gluten-free | Dairy-free | Vegetarian | Vegan | Nut-free | Egg-free

Prep Time | 25 minutes

Cook Time | 22 minutes

Makes | 9 or 10 muffins

Trust me, you're going to want to keep this recipe in your back pocket. Use it to create basic allergy-friendly muffins, or mix and match your favorite add-ins and flavors to make it your own. No matter which one you choose, you can't go wrong!

DRY

2 cups (195–200 g) Oat Flour (page 22)

1 teaspoon baking soda

½ teaspoon baking powder

¼ teaspoon kosher salt

⅓–½ cup (66–100 g) raw sugar (cane sugar) or fine coconut sugar

WET

⅔ cup (160 ml) nondairy milk, at room temperature or warm

3 tablespoons (45 ml) naturally refined coconut oil or avocado oil

1 tablespoon (15 ml) fresh lemon juice or 2 teaspoons (10 ml) apple cider vinegar

2 tablespoons (40 g) maple syrup or honey

1. Preheat the oven to 350°F (175°C). Line a 12-count muffin tin with liners and/or spray with cooking spray.
2. In a large mixing bowl, sift together the dry ingredients. In a large measuring cup, whisk together the wet ingredients. Set aside and let sit for 10 minutes. Working in batches, gently combine the wet ingredients into the dry ingredients until well mixed.
3. **To make the blueberry oat:** Fold in the berries and oats (if using).
   To make the chocolate chip: Fold in the chocolate chips and vanilla.
   To make the lemon poppy seed: Mix in the additional lemon juice, poppy seeds, zest, and cinnamon (if using). Add lemon slices (if using) to the top of each muffin right before baking.
4. Let the batter sit for 10 minutes, then divide it evenly among 9 or 10 muffin cups, filling each three-quarters full. Bake for 20 to 24 minutes, or until a toothpick inserted into the center comes out clean.
5. Remove from the oven and let cool in the muffin tin for 5 minutes. Remove the muffins to a cooling rack to finish cooling before serving.

Notes
- If using coconut oil, use warm milk so the coconut oil won't solidify. If using avocado oil, use milk at cold or room temperature.
- See page 166 for dairy-free chocolate chips suggestions.

Storage
- Store in an airtight container in the fridge for up to 1 week, or freeze for up to 3 months.

BLUEBERRY OAT

⅓–½ cup (48–75 g) fresh or frozen blueberries

2 tablespoons (12 g) gluten-free old-fashioned rolled oats (optional)

CHOCOLATE CHIP

⅓–½ cup (58–87 g) dairy-free chocolate chips

1 teaspoon pure vanilla extract

LEMON POPPY SEED

2 tablespoons (30 ml) fresh lemon juice or 1 teaspoon (5 ml) lemon extract

3 tablespoons (27 g) poppy seeds

2–3 tablespoons (12–18 g) fresh lemon zest

Dash of ground cinnamon (optional)

Lemon slices, for garnish (optional)

CHOCOLATE PROTEIN MUFFINS

Gluten-free | Dairy-free | Vegetarian |
Vegan Option | Nut-free | Egg-free Option

Prep Time | 10 minutes

Cook Time | 15 minutes

Makes | 12 muffins

Have your chocolate and eat it, too, with these high-protein muffins! They're made with simple staples for a gluten-free and refined sugar–free breakfast or snack you can feel good about.

DRY

1¾ cups (195 g) Oat Flour (page 22)

⅓–½ cup (40–50 g) chocolate plant-based protein powder

1 tablespoon (5 g) cocoa powder

2 teaspoons (9 g) baking powder

½ teaspoon baking soda

¼ teaspoon kosher salt

WET

3 tablespoons (45 ml) naturally refined coconut oil or avocado oil

¼–⅓ cup (85–115 g) maple syrup or honey

⅔ cup (160 ml) nondairy milk, at room temperature

2 eggs, at room temperature, or 1 small banana, mashed (108–112 g)

1 teaspoon pure vanilla extract

½ cup (87 g) dairy-free dark chocolate chips

1. Preheat the oven to 350°F (175°C). Line a 12-count muffin tin with liners or spray generously with cooking spray.
2. In a mixing bowl, sift together the dry ingredients. In another large bowl, whisk together the wet ingredients. Gently combine the wet ingredients into the dry ingredients. Fold in the chocolate chips.
3. Spoon the batter into the lined muffin pan, filling the cups two-thirds to three-quarters full. Bake the muffins for 15 to 18 minutes, or until a toothpick inserted into the center comes out clean. Remove from the oven and let cool in the muffin tin for 5 minutes. Remove the muffins to a cooling rack to finish cooling before serving.

Notes
- If using coconut oil, use warm milk so the coconut oil won't solidify. If using avocado oil, use milk at cold or room temperature.
- For an egg-free option, omit the eggs and use the banana option listed in the ingredient list.
- For a vegan option, use maple syrup instead of honey and banana instead of eggs.
- See pages 166 to 167 for soy-free vegan butter, sugar substitute, and plant-based protein powder suggestions.

Storage
- Store in an airtight container in the fridge for up to 1 week, or freeze for up to 3 months.

TRAIL MIX BREAKFAST COOKIES

Gluten-free | Grain-free | Dairy-free |
Vegan | Vegetarian | Nut-free | Egg-free

Prep Time | 10 minutes

Cook Time | 7 to 9 minutes

Makes | 15 to 18 cookies

Inspired by trail mix packets, these breakfast cookies feature fruits, seeds, and protein for a nut-free breakfast cookie that's great for taking on the go. Mix and match your favorite add-ins for a breakfast recipe that's truly your own.

1 cup (110–120 g) raw pumpkin seeds (pepitas) or sunflower seeds

½ cup (75 g) pitted dates (10–12 dates)

1 small ripe banana (80 g)

1 tablespoon (15 ml) naturally refined coconut oil or avocado oil

⅓–½ cup (40–50 g) plant-based protein powder (plain, vanilla, or chocolate)

1 teaspoon pure vanilla extract

¼ teaspoon kosher salt

1–2 tablespoons mix-ins of choice

½ cup (87 g) dairy-free dark chocolate chips (optional)

MIX-INS

Shredded unsweetened coconut

Dried cranberries

Chocolate chips

1. Preheat the oven to 350°F (175°C). Line a sheet pan with parchment paper.
2. In a food processor bowl, place the pumpkin seeds and dates. Blend until a gritty-like texture is formed. It will be a little sticky. Add the banana and coconut oil. Blend on high speed until a gritty thick batter is formed.
3. Transfer the batter to a large mixing bowl. Add the protein powder, vanilla, and salt. Mix with a rubber spatula. Fold in the mix-ins. The batter should be thick (like cookie dough batter). If it is soft, roll into a ball and place in the fridge to chill for 45 minutes or in the freezer for 15 minutes.
4. When the batter is thick enough to scoop, roll the dough into golf-ball-size balls (22 to 25 g each) and place on the prepared sheet pan. Do not press flat yet.
5. Bake the cookies in the ball shape for 7 to 9 minutes (9 minutes for crispier edges). Remove from the oven and gently press each cookie using the back of an oiled flat-bottomed measuring cup. Let cool for 5 minutes on the sheet pan before transferring to a cooling rack.
6. While the cookies cool, if desired, melt the dark chocolate in the microwave or in a double boiler. Dip one half of each cookie in the chocolate or drizzle it on top. Let the chocolate harden before serving.

Note
- For the best texture, use a protein powder containing pea protein. See page 167 for protein powder suggestions.

Storage
- Store leftovers in an airtight container for up to 5 days, or freeze for up to 2 months.

CUSTOMIZABLE CHIA PUDDING CUPS

Gluten-free | Dairy-free | Vegetarian |
Vegan | Nut-free | Egg-free

Prep Time | 15 minutes

Fridge Time | 1 hour to 24 hours

Makes | 2 or 3 servings

Add these chia pudding cups to your weekly meal prep for a grab-and-go option loaded with fiber, protein, and nutrients to keep you fueled all morning long! Customize the ingredients to make them your own.

1–2 cups (weight varies) sliced fresh or frozen fruit, such as berries, frozen peaches, and/or banana

1 cup (235 ml) nondairy milk

2 tablespoons (40 g) maple syrup or honey

¼–⅓ cup (44–60 g) chia seeds

Pinch of ground cinnamon

⅓–½ cup (40–50 g) plant-based vanilla protein powder (optional)

2 tablespoons (14 g) hemp seeds (optional)

TOPPINGS (OPTIONAL)

⅓ cup (67 g) nondairy yogurt

Sliced fruit

Chopped fresh mint

1. Place the fruit, milk, and maple syrup in a blender or food processor. Blend until a smoothie-like texture is formed. Alternatively, if you don't have a blender, finely chop the fruit and mix the ingredients until well combined.
2. Transfer the blended mixture to a large bowl or divide into 2 or 3 meal prep jars. Mix in the chia seeds, about 2 tablespoons (22 g) per jar.
3. Stir in the cinnamon, protein powder (if using), and hemp seeds (if using). Cover and place in the fridge for 1 hour or up to 24 hours. Overnight will result in an extra-thick protein pudding.
4. Top each serving with your desired toppings (if using).

Notes
- To help thicken the chia pudding without protein powder, mix in 2 to 3 tablespoons (12 to 18 g) gluten-free, old-fashioned rolled oats or steel-cut oats.
- See page 167 for plant-based protein powder suggestions.

Storage
- Store in an airtight container in the fridge for up to 5 days, or freeze for up to 2 weeks.

EGG BREAKFAST WRAPS

Gluten-free | Grain-free | Dairy-free | Vegetarian | Nut-free

Prep Time | 5 minutes

Cook Time | 5 minutes

Makes | 6 wraps

These quick and easy egg wraps are low in carbs and high in protein, and they're also super fun to customize with all your favorite add-ins. They're guaranteed to please even the pickiest of eaters!

2–3 teaspoons (10–15 ml) naturally refined coconut oil or avocado oil or soy-free vegan butter, melted

6 large eggs

FILLINGS

Herbs

Salsa

Egg-Free Mayo (page 41)

Sliced avocado

Breakfast Sausage Bites (page 62)

1. In a medium nonstick skillet over medium-high heat, add 1 teaspoon of the oil.
2. In a small bowl, whisk one egg, then gently pour into the hot pan. Swirl the pan to evenly spread the egg into a thin layer, similar to cooking an omelet. The thinner the egg layer, the better it will work for an egg wrap.
3. Cook the egg for 1 to 3 minutes, or until the edges start to turn golden brown and the middle is set, then carefully flip the egg wrap over. Continue to cook for 1 to 3 minutes, until the egg is fully cooked in the middle. Remove the egg wrap and set on a plate to cool.
4. Repeat with the remaining eggs, cooking one egg at a time. Use additional oil as needed to keep the pan slick.
5. Once all the wraps are made, fill each with the desired fillings, then roll them up tightly and wrap in foil or parchment paper. If desired, brush a little oil onto the inside of the foil or parchment to keep the egg wraps fresh.

Note
- See page 166 for soy-free vegan butter suggestions.

Storage
- Store in an airtight container or wrapped in foil in the fridge for up to 5 days. To freeze, place a piece of parchment paper or wax paper between egg wraps and freeze for up to 3 months. Do not fill the wraps before freezing.

CHICKPEA CREPES/WRAPS

Gluten-free | Dairy-free | Vegetarian |
Vegan | Nut-free | Egg-free

Prep Time | 2 minutes

Rest Time | 30 minutes

Cook Time | 6 minutes per crepe

Makes | 5 to 7 crepes

These are just as light and fluffy as traditional crepes with none of the eggs or gluten. This version is made with chickpea flour for a high-protein option the whole family will love. Load them up with all your favorite fillings for a sweet or savory breakfast or brunch.

1¼ cups (150 g) chickpea flour

⅓ cup (80 ml) nondairy milk

1 cup (235 ml) water

¼ teaspoon kosher salt

1 tablespoon (15 ml) naturally refined coconut oil or avocado oil, plus more as needed

1. In a high-speed blender, add the chickpea flour, milk, water, and salt. Blend for 30 seconds, or until creamy and smooth. Let sit at room temperature for 30 minutes to thicken.
2. Warm a 10- to 12-inch (25 to 30 cm) crepe pan (recommended) or nonstick frying pan over medium-high heat. Grease with the oil, brushing with a spatula to coat evenly.
3. Scoop ⅓ cup (80 ml) of the batter and pour into the pan. Lift the pan and swiftly rotate to distribute the batter evenly across the bottom, adding more batter if needed. The batter will be very liquidy. The thickness of the crepes will depend on how much batter is added to the pan.
4. Cook for 2 to 3 minutes, then flip gently. Continue to cook for 1 minute, or until golden brown. Repeat until all the batter is used up, adding more oil as needed.

Notes
- The batter can be made 1 to 2 days ahead. Be sure to cover and keep it in the fridge.
- The batter must be thin to coat the pan and cook evenly. Thicker batter will result in a more pancake-like texture and will cook differently. For the best results, use a crepe pan.

Storage
- Store leftovers in the fridge in an airtight container with a piece of parchment paper between crepes to prevent sticking.

PLANT-POWERED PROTEIN PANCAKES

Gluten-free | Dairy-free | Vegetarian |
Vegan | Nut-free | Egg-free

Prep Time | 15 minutes

Cook Time | 5 minutes

Makes | 5 to 7 pancakes

Give your weekend pancakes an upgrade with this plant-based recipe! Millet flour is combined with minimal ingredients and plant-based protein for a hearty texture and truly magical taste.

1⅓ cups (325 ml) nondairy milk

1 tablespoon (15 ml) distilled white vinegar or apple cider vinegar

¼ teaspoon pure vanilla extract (optional)

1 ¾–2 cups (240 g) Millet Flour (page 24)

⅓–½ cup (40–50 g) plant-based protein powder

2 teaspoons (9 g) baking powder

1 teaspoon baking soda

3–4 tablespoons (39–50 g) raw sugar (cane sugar) or monk fruit sweetener

1 tablespoon (15 ml) naturally refined coconut oil or avocado oil, plus more as needed

1. In a small bowl, combine the milk with the vinegar and vanilla (if using). Set aside for 5 to 10 minutes to create "buttermilk."
2. In a large mixing bowl, sift or whisk together the flour, protein powder, baking powder, baking soda, and sugar. Once the milk has curdled, pour it into the bowl with the dry ingredients. Whisk to combine, being careful not to overmix. Let the batter rest for 10 to 15 minutes.
3. Heat a griddle over low to medium heat, and grease with 1 teaspoon of the coconut oil, brushing with a spatula to coat evenly.
4. Using a ¼- or ⅓-cup (60 or 80 g) measuring cup, add the batter to the hot griddle. Heat for 2 to 3 minutes, or until small bubbles begin to form on top. Using a spatula, flip the pancakes over. Cook for 2 to 3 minutes, or until golden.
5. Repeat until all the remaining pancake batter is used up, adding more oil as needed. Serve the pancakes warm.

Note
- See page 167 for plant-based protein powder suggestions.

Storage
- Store leftovers in an airtight container in the fridge for up to 4 days. Freeze cooled pancakes in an airtight container for up to 3 months.

BREAKFAST SAUSAGE BITES

Gluten-free | Dairy-free | Nut-free |
Egg-free

Prep Time | 10 minutes

Cook Time | 10 to 12 minutes

Makes | 17 to 20 bites

Better than your local diner's, this recipe is made with simple spices and just a touch of honey or maple syrup for the perfect balance of sweet and spicy. Pop them in the air fryer or oven for a quick bite-size breakfast protein!

1 pound (454 g) ground sausage
of choice

2 teaspoons (6 g) minced garlic

⅓ cup (55 g) chopped yellow onion

2 teaspoons (1 g) fresh thyme leaves
or ½ teaspoon dried thyme

¼ teaspoon smoked paprika or
cayenne pepper

¼ teaspoon kosher salt

¼ teaspoon black pepper

2 teaspoons (10 ml) maple syrup
or (14 g) honey

Sauce of choice, for serving

1. Line a sheet pan with parchment paper. In a large bowl, combine all the ingredients. Using two hands, mix the ingredients together until well blended. Shape the sausage mixture into patties about 1½ inches (4 cm) wide and 1½ inches (4 cm) thick. Place the patties on the sheet pan.

To air fry:
1. Preheat the air fryer to 375°F (190°C). Once preheated, spray the air fryer basket with cooking spray.
2. Place 5 or 6 patties in the air fryer basket. Air fry for 10 to 12 minutes, flipping halfway through cooking. Check for doneness at 10 to 12 minutes with an internal temperature of 165°F (74°C).
3. Remove the sausage patties from the air fryer, place on a clean plate, and cover to keep warm. Repeat to air fry the remaining patties.
4. Serve with your sauce of choice.

To bake:
1. Preheat the oven to 375°F (190°C).
2. Place the sausage patties on a parchment-lined sheet pan and bake for 20 to 22 minutes, flipping halfway through. The internal temperature should reach 165°F (74°C).
3. Optional: Remove the parchment paper and place the sausage patties back on the sheet pan. Turn the oven to broil, and broil the patties for 1 to 2 minutes for extra crispy edges.

Note
- See page 167 for gluten-free sausage suggestions.

Storage
- Store leftovers in an airtight container in the fridge for up to 4 days.

- To freeze, place in a freezer-friendly container and freeze for up to 3 months.

THE GLUTEN-FREE FAMILY COOKBOOK

POTATO WAFFLES

Gluten-free | Grain-free | Dairy-free |
Vegetarian | Nut-free | Egg-free

Prep Time | 15 minutes

Cook Time | 3 to 5 minutes per waffle

Makes | 2 or 3 waffles

One bite of these potato waffles and you'll kiss the store-bought options goodbye! All you need are potatoes and spices to create a hearty, fiber-loaded, plant-based recipe. Pair this recipe with Sheet-Pan Coconut Crust Chicken (page 118).

2–3 medium russet potatoes, peeled and washed (500–600 g)

½ teaspoon onion powder

½ teaspoon garlic powder

¼ teaspoon smoked or regular paprika

¼ teaspoon kosher salt

¼ teaspoon pepper

2–3 tablespoons (10–15 g) nutritional yeast or Parmesan cheese (optional)

Avocado oil cooking spray

1. Steam the potatoes in the microwave or roast until tender. (See Notes.)
2. Place the steamed and softened potatoes in a food processor with the grate attachment. Grate the potatoes until they resemble "rice" or hash browns. Alternatively, you can use a cheese grater to grate the potatoes.
3. Add the potatoes, onion powder, garlic powder, paprika, salt, pepper, and nutritional yeast (if using) to a mixing bowl. Toss together to mix.
4. Preheat a waffle iron. When the waffle iron is hot, spray both sides generously with high heat avocado oil cooking spray. Place a generous ¼ to ⅓ cup (60 to 80 g) of potato mixture on each of the four waffle divisions; the amount may vary depending on the size of your waffle iron. Spread the batter evenly. Cook for 3 to 5 minutes, or until the potatoes are browned and crispy; the time may vary depending on the size of the waffle iron. Remove the cooked waffle and repeat until all the batter is used up.

Notes
- I recommend using russet potatoes; sweet potatoes are too starchy and will burn faster.
- To steam potatoes in the microwave: Pierce each potato, skin-on, multiple times with a fork. Place the potatoes on a microwave-safe plate. For 2 medium-size potatoes, microwave on high for 10 to 12 minutes. The time depends on the size of the potatoes. Check the tenderness at 8 minutes and adjust the cook time as needed. The potatoes are done cooking when tender yet firm enough to hold their shape. Don't let the potatoes get too soft. Remove the hot potatoes with a dish towel or an oven mitt.
- Transfer the potatoes to a sheet pan lined with parchment paper and keep warm in the oven at 200°F (93°C) until ready to serve or for up to 30 minutes.

Storage
- Place leftovers in an airtight container or wrap individually in foil and store in the fridge for up to 2 days.

4 { Smoothies

Smoothies are a staple in my day-to-day routine, and with a little trial and error, I've nailed the perfect formula to create the best taste and texture every time. Take a look at my go-to smoothies, find the best add-ins for a boost of nutrients, and learn how to make your own creations with ease.

I used nutrient-rich superfood ingredients to create eight tasty smoothie recipes to boost brain function, improve gut health, and keep you feeling full! Follow my recipes, or use the formulas and pairing suggestions to create your own.

(top and left) Brain Booster Smoothie, page 73
(bottom and right) Hidden Veggie Smoothie, page 70

Welcome to the smoothie section!

In the following pages, I'll share our best tips, tricks, and recipes to create nutritious and delicious smoothies for all your needs. To get started, I've provided a list of my favorite go-to ingredients to keep on hand for tasty smoothies in a pinch. Use the ingredients below as a foundation for your own smoothie creations. Or, keep reading to learn how I use them in my daily recipes!

- **Honey—Add to smoothies with less sweet fruits (such as citrus) or veggies.**

- **Ginger—A little goes a long way for a bit of zing! Pair with all your favorite fruits, including banana, mango, apples, pears, pineapple, and oranges.**

- **Leafy Greens—Combine with sweet fruits, such as bananas or berries.**

- **Blendable Vegetables—Combine frozen and blendable veggies, such as cauliflower and zucchini, with all your favorite fruits for a flavorless nutrient boost.**

- **Citrus—Mix and match your favorite citrus with any fruit you'd like for a refreshing flavor.**

- **Berries—Pair with all your favorite fruit along with herbs and spices such as mint, basil, and cinnamon.**

- **Banana—Pair with all your favorite ingredients for a boost of sweetness and an extra thick texture without the need for refined sugar.**

- **Flaxseed and Chia Seeds—Add to all your favorite smoothies for a boost of omega-3 fatty acids and plant-based protein.**

- **Avocado—Combine with sweet fruits, such as bananas and berries, for an extra creamy texture.**

- **Kiwi—Pairs well with sweet fruits, such as strawberries, mango, and banana.**

HIDDEN VEGGIE SMOOTHIE

Gluten-free | Grain-free | Dairy-free | Nut-free | Egg-free

Prep Time | 5 minutes

Makes | 1 or 2 servings

Get your daily dose of veggies without even trying. Spinach is an extremely nutrient-rich vegetable! Blend baby spinach right into smoothies for a boost in plant-based iron and calcium. Zucchini can be peeled and frozen to create a high-volume recipe that's full of antioxidants and fiber. Cherries are especially rich in vitamin C, potassium, and fiber and contain powerful anti-inflammatory compounds for a superfood that makes your smoothies extra pretty.

1 cup (235 ml) coconut milk

1 cup (235 ml) orange juice

1 cup (120 g) chopped zucchini

1 cup (155 g) pitted cherries and/or berries

½ cup (15 g) baby spinach

1 tablespoon (12 g) whole flaxseed

Ground cinnamon, to taste

Kosher salt, to taste

Honey or maple syrup, to taste (optional)

1. Add all the ingredients to a high-speed blender. Blend until smooth. If the smoothie is too thick, add more liquid (¼ cup [60 ml] at a time) as needed. Pour into a tall glass and serve.

Notes
- Flaxseeds are included to improve the texture of the smoothie and contain vitamins, nutrients, and healthy fats that contribute to proper energy metabolism, cell function, brain health, and immune system functioning.
- For creamy cold smoothies, freeze canned coconut milk or cream for 24 hours. Remove and spoon the solid portion into the blender. Reserve leftover coconut water to add to other smoothies.

PROTEIN POWER SMOOTHIE

Gluten-free | Grain-free | Dairy-free |
Vegetarian | Vegan | Egg-free | Nut-free

Prep Time | 5 minutes

Makes | 1 or 2 servings

A delicious way to pump up your protein. Plant-based protein powder or collagen peptides can be included to turn any smoothie into a complete meal. I recommend using a neutral flavor or unflavored version so as not to overpower the rest of the ingredients. Unsweetened cocoa powder is a great way to add an indulgent chocolate taste, and it is loaded with polyphenols and antioxidants.

2 cups (510 g) frozen strawberries

½–1 cup (66–132 g) frozen cauliflower florets

1 tablespoon (16 g) Sunflower Seed Butter (page 42)

¼ cup (25 g) plant-based protein powder

1–2 tablespoons (5–10 g) unsweetened cocoa powder

1–1½ cups (235–355 ml) nondairy milk

Ground cinnamon, to taste

Kosher salt, to taste

Raw honey or maple syrup, to taste (optional)

1. Add all the ingredients to a high-speed blender. Blend until smooth. If the smoothie is too thick, add more liquid (¼ cup [60 ml] at a time) as needed. Pour into a tall glass and serve.

Notes
- Frozen cauliflower is virtually flavorless and can be used to bulk up the volume of your smoothies while adding a boost of vitamin C and fiber.
- See page 167 for protein powder suggestions.

GOOD GUT SMOOTHIE

Gluten-free | Grain-free | Dairy-free | Nut-free | Vegetarian

Prep Time | 5 minutes

Makes | 1 or 2 servings

Boost your digestion with ease. Gingerroot has been used all around the world to help aid digestion and reduce nausea. It's a powerful ingredient that's soothing to eat! Collagen peptides are a great source of protein that is naturally found in the body and used to help improve gut, skin, and hair health. Chia seeds are a mighty little ingredient that's packed with fiber to assist the digestive process and keep your body regular.

1 cup (235 ml) coconut milk

1 kiwi, peeled

1–1½ cups (165–250 g) chopped pineapple

½ banana (optional)

1 teaspoon grated fresh ginger, or to taste

1 serving (10–20 g) collagen peptides

1 teaspoon grated fresh ginger, or to taste

1 teaspoon (4 g) spirulina powder (optional)

1 tablespoon (11 g) chia seeds (optional)

1. Add all the ingredients to a high-speed blender. Blend until smooth. If the smoothie is too thick, add more liquid (¼ cup [60 ml] at a time) as needed. Pour into a tall glass and serve.

Notes
- For a thicker smoothie, use frozen fruit and add more liquid as needed.
- Add spirulina powder for healthy benefits and a vibrant green smoothie.
- See page 167 for collagen peptides suggestions.

BRAIN BOOSTER SMOOTHIE

Gluten-free | Grain-free | Dairy-free |
Nut-free | Egg-free | Vegetarian Option

Prep Time | 5 minutes

Makes | 1 or 2 servings

A superfood drink for clearer thinking! Hemp milk is a great alternative to dairy-based milk and is naturally higher in plant-based proteins and healthy fats than other nondairy milks. In fact, it's the only option that contains all nine essential amino acids, making it a complete source of protein! Avocado can help create a smooth, creamy texture while also contributing a great source of healthy monounsaturated fats and vitamins that can contribute to brain health.

1½ cups (355 ml) Hemp Seed Milk (page 26)

1 cup (30 g) baby spinach

1 cup (145 g) blueberries

1–2 tablespoons (11–22 g) chia seeds or whole flaxseed

¼ cup (38 g) diced avocado

Raw honey or maple syrup, to taste

½–1 ounce (14–28 g) collagen peptides, hemp protein, or a seed-based protein

1. Add all the ingredients to a high-speed blender. Blend until smooth. If the smoothie is too thick, add more liquid (¼ cup [60 ml] at a time) as needed. Pour into a tall glass and serve.

Notes
- Blueberries are one of the most highly rated superfoods! Use them to pack in tons of antioxidants, fiber, and a hint of sweetness.
- For a creamy texture, freeze sliced fruit and avocado in an ice cube tray. Cover each cube with nondairy milk and freeze until solid. Remove from the tray when ready to blend.
- See page 167 for collagen peptide and protein powder suggestions.

BERRY BALANCED SMOOTHIE

Gluten-free | Grain-free | Dairy-free |
Nut-free | Vegetarian

Prep Time | 5 minutes

Makes | 1 or 2 servings

Who said balanced meals must be complicated? This recipe has a balance of the macronutrients and antioxidants you need to fuel your day! Blueberries are one of the most highly rated superfoods! Use them to pack in tons of antioxidants, fiber, and a hint of sweetness.

1–1 ½ cups (235–355 ml) nondairy milk

2 cups frozen mixed berries

½–1 small banana (40–80 g)

¼ cup (25 g) plant-based vanilla protein powder

1 tablespoon Sunflower Seed Butter (page 42)

2 tablespoons gluten-free oats (optional)

Ground cinnamon, to taste

Raw honey or maple syrup, to taste

1. Add all the ingredients to a high-speed blender. Blend until smooth. If the smoothie is too thick, add more liquid (¼ cup [60 ml] at a time) as needed. Pour into a tall glass and serve.

Notes
- For a thicker smoothie, freeze the fruit and add more liquid as needed.
- See page 167 for protein powder suggestions and page 166 for gluten-free oat suggestions.

GOOD TO THE BONE SMOOTHIE

Gluten-free | Grain-free | Dairy-free | Nut-free | Egg-free

Prep Time | 5 minutes

Makes | 1 or 2 servings

Better than a glass of milk, this smoothie is packed with bone-building nutrients! Collagen has many important functions and health benefits, such as improving skin structure and strengthening your bones. The pitted dates in this smoothie also contain calcium and phosphorus, which helps your bones absorb more minerals.

2 cups (300 g) fresh or frozen blackberries or blueberries

1 to 2 servings (11–22 g) chocolate or vanilla collagen peptides

1¼ cups (300 ml) almond milk or Hemp Seed Milk (page 26)

¼ cup (60 g) coconut milk yogurt or nondairy vanilla yogurt of choice

3–4 pitted dates

⅓ cup (22 g) chopped curly kale (optional)

1 tablespoon (11 g) chia seeds or whole flaxseeds

Raw honey or maple syrup, to taste

Pinch of sea salt (optional)

1. Add all the ingredients to a high-speed blender. Blend until smooth. Pour into a tall glass and serve.

Notes
- For a thicker smoothie, freeze the fruit and add more liquid as needed.
- For better calcium absorption, lightly soften/steam the kale before blending.
- See page 167 for collagen peptides suggestions.

SUNNY C SMOOTHIE

Gluten-free | Grain-free | Dairy-free |
Vegetarian | Nut-free | Egg-free

Prep Time | 5 minutes

Makes | 1 or 2 servings

*Inspired by your favorite childhood drink but without all the processed ingredients!
This antioxidant-rich smoothie is perfect for keeping our immune system in check.
You'll get your daily Vitamin C needs and it's anti-inflammatory thanks to the touch
of turmeric!*

1¼ cups (190g) frozen mango and/or
pineapple chunks

½ cup (120ml) fresh orange juice

⅓ – ½ cup (50-75g) sliced frozen
banana

1¼ cups (300g) coconut milk or
nondairy milk of choice

1 tablespoon (12 g) whole flaxseed or
chia seed

2 teaspoons (10 ml) fresh lime juice

Pinch of ground turmeric, to taste and
for anti-inflammatory boost

Honey or maple syrup, to taste (optional)

¼ cup (60 ml) chilled canned coconut
milk or nondairy yogurt of choice,
to thicken (optional)

1. Add all the ingredients to a high-speed blender. Blend until smooth. If the
   smoothie is too thick, add more liquid (¼ cup [60 ml] at a time) as needed.
   Pour into a tall glass and serve.

Note

- For creamy cold smoothies, freeze canned coconut milk or cream for 24 hours.
  Remove and spoon the solid portion into the blender. Reserve leftover coconut
  water to add to other smoothies, like the Power Green Smoothie (page 77)!

POWER GREEN SMOOTHIE

Gluten-free | Grain-free | Dairy-free |
Vegetarian | Vegan | Nut-free | Egg-free

Prep Time | 5 minutes

Makes | 1 or 2 servings

Get your greens on! Packed with vitamins, nutrients, and fiber, this smoothie will help you power through even the longest of days feeling fueled and energized. Fruit high in vitamin C (such as orange and mango) aid in plant-based iron absorption, which you get from the spinach.

1 cup (150 g) frozen mango chunks

1 banana, fresh or frozen

2 cups (60 g) baby spinach

1–1¼ cups (235–355 ml) nondairy milk

⅓ cup (80 ml) fresh squeezed orange juice or coconut water

1 tablespoon (8 g) whole flaxseeds

Raw honey or maple syrup, to taste (optional)

1. Add all the ingredients to a high-speed blender. Blend until smooth. If the smoothie is too thick, add more liquid (¼ cup [60 ml] at a time) as needed. Pour into a tall glass and serve.

5 Snack Hacks

Whether you need something on the savory side or are craving a little sweetness in your life, I've got you covered with quick, creative, grab-and-go bites and after-school allergy-friendly snacks. Everything is homemade and healthy for when you get that snack attack.

Crispy Chickpeas, page 90

SUPERFOOD PROTEIN BARS

Gluten-free | Dairy-free | Vegetarian | Vegan | Nut-free | Egg-free

Prep Time | 5 minutes

Cook Time | 15 minutes

Makes | 9 to 12 bars

Skip the checkout line and make your own protein bars at home instead! Budget-friendly and made with natural ingredients, this version is better for you but tastier than anything you'll find in the store.

1 cup (80 g) gluten-free quick-cooking oats

1 cup (100 g) chocolate or vanilla plant-based protein powder

⅓–½ cup (80–120 ml) maple syrup or agave syrup

⅓–½ cup (42–63 g) flax meal or chia seeds

1 cup (235 ml) nondairy milk

¼ teaspoon kosher salt

1 teaspoon pure vanilla extract

½–1 cup (75–145 g) fresh blueberries or raspberries (optional)

1. Preheat the oven to 350°F (175°C) and line an 8 x 8-inch (20 x 20 cm) baking pan with parchment paper.
2. Combine all the ingredients except for the berries in a large mixing bowl. Gently fold in the berries. Press the mixture evenly and firmly into the prepared baking pan.
3. Bake for 15 to 18 minutes, or until just golden around the edges. Remove from the oven and let cool completely before cutting into bars.

Note
- See page 167 for plant-based protein powder suggestions.

Storage
- Store the bars in an airtight container in the fridge for 7 to 10 days.

NO-BAKE APPLE CINNAMON ENERGY BITES

Gluten-free | Dairy-free | Vegetarian | Vegan | Nut-free | Egg-free

Prep Time | 15 minutes

Cook Time | 15 minutes

Makes | 25 to 28 bites

When it comes to nutritious recipes that can be prepped in advance, no-bake bites have been my go-to for years. These are plant-based and nut-free, and they use household staples for nutrient-dense snacks that the kids will love to make!

5 ounces (140 g) dried unsulfured apple rings (about 8 apple rings)

2 cups (200 g) roasted unsalted sunflower seeds

2 tablespoons (16 g) whole flaxseed

¼ cup (65 g) Sunflower Seed Butter (page 42)

6 tablespoons (90 ml) maple syrup or (120 g) honey

1 tablespoon (7 g) ground cinnamon

¼ cup (25 g) plant-based protein powder or 3 tablespoons (18 g) Oat Flour (page 22), plus more if needed

1. In a food processor bowl or high-speed blender, add the apple rings, sunflower seeds, and flaxseed. Pulse until a mealy texture is formed.
2. Transfer the apple mixture to a large bowl and add the sunflower seed butter, maple syrup, cinnamon, and protein powder. Gently stir to combine.
3. Adjust the amount of maple syrup or honey needed for the batter to stick together. If the batter is too sticky, add 1 to 3 tablespoons (6 to 18 g) of oat flour and mix together. Chill in the refrigerator to firm up.
4. Remove the batter from the fridge and roll into 1- to 1½-inch (2.5 to 4 cm) balls (18 to 20 g each). Place the balls on a plate or tray.
5. Chill in the refrigerator for 15 minutes, or until firm.

Note
- See page 167 for plant-based protein powder suggestions.

Storage
- Store leftovers in an airtight container in the fridge for up to 2 weeks, or freeze for up to 3 months.

CHOCOLATE COCONUT PROTEIN BALLS

Gluten-free | Dairy-free | Vegetarian |
Vegan Option | Egg-free |
Nut-free Option

Prep Time | 25 minutes

Cook Time | 30 to 35 minutes

Makes | 12 to 14 balls

Rich in flavor and nutrients, these little bites pack in healthy fats and protein while still being low in sugar. Make them for a quick snack or dessert. No baking required.

⅓ cup (42 g) flax meal

2 tablespoons (10 g) unsweetened cocoa powder

¼ cup (65 g) almond butter or Sunflower Seed Butter (page 42)

2 tablespoons (30 ml) maple syrup or (40 g) honey (optional)

½ cup (50 g) chocolate plant-based protein powder of choice

1–2 tablespoons (14–28 g) coconut oil, solidified

⅓ cup (28 g) unsweetened shredded coconut, plus more to coat

2–3 tablespoons (22–33 g) dairy-free dark chocolate morsels

1. Place the flax meal and cocoa powder in a food processor. Blend until combined.
2. Add the almond butter, maple syrup (if using), protein powder, coconut oil, and coconut. Blend until a smooth batter is formed. This might take a couple of minutes, so be sure to stop the food processor or blender and scrape down the sides as needed.
3. Transfer the batter to a large mixing bowl and fold in the chocolate. Roll the batter into one large ball, cover with plastic wrap, and place in the fridge to firm up for 20 to 30 minutes, or until the batter is firm enough to roll into balls.
4. Remove the batter from the fridge and line a sheet pan or shallow container with wax paper. Roll the dough into equal-size balls, about the size of golf balls, roll in shredded coconut to coat, and then place on the prepared sheet pan. Transfer the balls to the freezer for 15 to 20 minutes.

Notes
- If you don't have a blender, mix the batter by hand in a mixing bowl. Add the maple syrup to bind it together. The texture will be more gritty. Adjust the syrup depending on the thickness of the batter and amount of protein powder used.
- See page 167 for plant-based protein powder suggestions.

Storage
- Store leftovers in an airtight container in the fridge for up to 2 weeks, or freeze for up to 3 months.

CHEWY CEREAL BARS

Gluten-free | Dairy-free | Vegetarian | Vegan Option | Nut-free Option | Egg-free

Prep Time	10 minutes
Cook Time	5 minutes
Chill Time	30 minutes
Makes	9 to 12 bars

Half bar, half better-for-you Krispie treat, these bars were an accidental recipe that turned out to be great. They were concocted from a combination of leftover ingredients, and now they're a staple recipe that can be served for breakfast, snacks, dessert, and everything in between!

¾ cup (195 g) creamy almond butter or Sunflower Seed Butter (page 42)

⅔ cup (230 g) honey or agave syrup

½ cup (100 g) raw sugar (cane sugar) or coconut palm sugar

1 teaspoon pure vanilla extract

Pinch of sea salt

2 cups (170 g) unsweetened coconut flakes

2 cups (28 g) puffed rice, millet, or quinoa cereal

MIX-INS (OPTIONAL)

Dairy-free dark chocolate chips

Dried cherries

Dried cranberries

1. Line an 8 x 8-inch (20 x 20 cm) baking pan with parchment paper or spray it with cooking spray.
2. In a large saucepan over medium-low heat, whisk together the nut butter, honey, and sugar.
3. Heat the mixture until it comes to a boil, stirring constantly. Remove the saucepan from the heat. Stir in the vanilla and salt.
4. Working quickly, use a silicone spatula to gently stir in the coconut flakes and cereal. Mix until evenly coated with the nut butter mixture. Transfer the batter to the prepared baking pan. Gently press it down using a spatula or your hands.
5. Place the baking pan in the fridge to chill the mixture for 30 to 45 minutes. Remove from the fridge and cut into bars.

Notes
- For a coconut-free bar, omit the coconut and use slivered almonds or pecan halves.
- See page 166 for puffed rice, millet, or quinoa cereal suggestions.

Storage
- Store sliced bars in an airtight container in the pantry for up to 1 week or in the fridge for 2 weeks.

CHEESY SEEDY CRACKERS

Gluten-free | Grain-free | Dairy-free |
Vegetarian | Vegan | Nut-free | Egg-free

Prep Time | 15 minutes

Cook Time | 40 to 50 minutes

Makes | 30 to 40 crackers

Grain-free, nut-free, and seasoned with nutritional yeast, these crackers are a fun snack and loaded with flavor. They're perfect for dipping, dunking, and sandwiching with all your favorite meals.

⅓ cup (56 g) whole flaxseed

2 tablespoons (14 g) flax meal

½ cup (88 g) chia seeds

½ cup (70 g) raw pumpkin seeds

½ cup (73 g) raw sunflower seeds

1 teaspoon sea salt

3 tablespoons (15 g) nutritional yeast or hemp seeds

2–3 tablespoons (10–15 g) seasoning mix, such as taco, fajita, ranch, etc.

1 cup (235 ml) water

1. Preheat the oven to 350°F (175°C). Line a sheet pan with parchment paper.
2. In a large bowl, mix together the flaxseed, flax meal, chia seeds, pumpkin seeds, sunflower seeds, salt, nutritional yeast, and seasoning. Pour the water over the mixture. Let sit for 10 minutes to allow the flax meal and chia seeds to thicken, like a gel.
3. Once the seeds have thickened, use a rubber spatula or spoon to spread the mixture in an even layer onto the prepared sheet pan. Spread to ¼ inch (6 mm) thick or less.
4. Bake for 25 to 30 minutes. Remove from the oven and cut into even squares using a knife or pizza wheel. Flip the crackers over and bake for 15 to 25 minutes longer, or until golden brown and crispy. Transfer to a cooling rack to dry out/cool completely before serving or storing.

Notes
- If using hemp seeds instead of nutritional yeast, add an additional 2 teaspoons of flaxseed.
- If using premade seasonings, read the ingredient list for hidden ingredients. See page 167 for gluten-free seasoning suggestions.

Storage
- Store in an airtight container in the pantry for 7 to 10 days.

COLLAGEN FRUIT GUMMIES

Gluten-free | Grain-free | Dairy-free | Nut-free | Egg-free

Prep Time | 7 minutes

Cook Time | 5 minutes

Chill Time | 2 hours

Makes | About 64 gummies

If you're looking for sweet snacks that aren't loaded with refined sugar, this recipe is for you! Unlike packaged varieties, these gummies are made with fresh fruit and collagen to create all the sweet taste your kids love with all the nutrients and gut health benefits parents want, too.

2 cups (475 ml) fresh pineapple juice, coconut water, or orange juice

1 kiwi, peeled and sliced

1 cup (125 g) fresh raspberries

¼ cup (85 g) honey

½ cup (80 g) grass-fed gelatin powder

Grated fresh ginger (optional)

1. Place the juice, kiwi, raspberries, and honey in a blender. Blend until the ingredients are well combined.
2. Pour the blended mixture into a small saucepan. Heat the mixture over medium-low heat until it starts to simmer. Do not let it come to a boil!
3. Scatter the gelatin powder over the mixture, whisking continuously. If the mixture starts to clump after adding all of the gelatin, transfer it back to the blender (or use an immersion blender) and blend until smooth. Return the mixture to the saucepan and heat over low heat for 1 minute.
4. Working quickly but gently, pour the fruit juice mixture into molds or a lined 8 x 8-inch (20 x 20 cm) baking dish. Place the mixture in the fridge to chill for 2 hours or in the freezer for 30 minutes, until it is hardened.
5. Once hardened, pop the gummies out of the molds. Or, if using a baking dish, flip it over onto a cutting board and cut the gummies into 1-inch (2.5 cm) cubes.

Notes
- Use 100 percent fresh pineapple juice and 1 teaspoon grated fresh ginger to aid in digestion. Or try a combination of fresh fruit juices.
- See page 167 for grass-fed gelatin powder suggestions.

Storage
- Store leftovers in an airtight container in the refrigerator for up to 2 weeks.

MICROWAVE ENGLISH MUFFINS

Gluten-free | Dairy-free | Vegetarian |
Vegan | Nut-free | Egg-free

Prep Time | 5 minutes

Cook Time | 2 minutes

Makes | 1 English muffin

Six ingredients and two minutes are all you'll need to whip up this wholesome snack! Light and fluffy, this grain-free English muffin is super tasty on its own or even better when loaded with all your favorite toppings. Try the Easy English Muffin Pizza (page 100).

¼ cup (30 g) Oat Flour (page 22)

½ teaspoon aluminum-free baking powder

1 tablespoon (7 g) flax meal

⅛ teaspoon kosher salt

2 tablespoons (30 g) unsweetened applesauce

½ teaspoon distilled white vinegar or apple cider vinegar

1. Preheat the toaster or oven to 350°F (175°C).
2. In a bowl, mix together the oat flour, baking powder, flax meal, and salt. Add the applesauce and white vinegar. Mix together well.
3. Spray a ramekin with cooking spray. Press the batter into the bottom of the ramekin. Microwave on high for 2 minutes. Remove from the microwave and let cool completely, then remove from the ramekin.
4. Slice the English muffin in half and toast until golden and the edges are crispy.

Note
- To double the recipe, blend all the ingredients in a food processor or blender. Divide the batter between two ramekins.

CRISPY CHICKPEAS

Gluten-free | Grain-free | Dairy-free |
Vegetarian | Nut-free | Egg-free

Prep Time | 5 minutes

Cook Time | 12 minutes

Makes | 1½ cups (250 g)

Inspired by Goldfish crackers, these crispy chickpeas are a better-for-you treat. Made with minimal ingredients, they're great for topping soups and salads, and are perfectly poppable for an easy snack!

1 can (15 ounces, or 425 g) chickpeas, drained

2–3 teaspoons (10–15 ml) olive oil

½ teaspoon garlic powder

½ teaspoon onion powder

½ teaspoon dried oregano

¼ teaspoon smoked paprika

½ teaspoon kosher salt

½ teaspoon black pepper

1 tablespoon (5 g) nutritional yeast or grated Parmesan

1. Drain and rinse the chickpeas in a colander, pat them dry with a paper towel, and remove the loose skins. Let them dry out for 30 minutes or up to 24 hours. The drier the chickpeas, the crispier the result!
2. After the chickpeas have dried out, transfer them to a mixing bowl and drizzle with the olive oil. Set aside.

To air fry:

1. Preheat the air fryer to 400°F (200°C). If your air fryer does not have a preheat function, heat an empty basket at 400°F (200°C) for 2 minutes. Spray the air fryer basket with cooking spray and place the chickpeas in the basket. Cook for 10 minutes, shaking halfway to stir the chickpeas.
2. After 10 minutes, check the chickpeas for desired doneness. Doneness can vary depending on the air fryer. Usually an extra 2 to 3 minutes is needed for that golden brown and extra crispy texture (total cooking time is 12 to 13 minutes).
3. Quickly transfer the chickpeas back to the mixing bowl and toss with the spices and nutritional yeast. Enjoy hot for extra crispy texture.

To bake:

1. Preheat the oven to 400°F (200°C). Line a sheet pan with parchment paper.
2. Arrange the chickpeas in a single layer on the prepared sheet pan. Bake for 25 to 30 minutes, shaking the pan every 10 minutes, until golden brown and crisp. If needed, keep roasting 5 to 10 minutes longer, keeping an eye on doneness.
3. Remove the pan from the oven, quickly transfer the chickpeas back to the mixing bowl, and toss with the spices and nutritional yeast. Enjoy hot for extra crispy texture.

Storage

- Store in a loosely covered container in the pantry for up to 5 days. If the seasoned chickpeas lose crispiness, simply reheat in the oven or air fryer at 400°F (200°C) for 2 to 3 minutes to crisp them up again.

COCONUT FLOUR TORTILLA/FLATBREAD

Gluten-free | Grain-free | Dairy-free |
Vegetarian | Vegan | Nut-free | Egg-free

Prep Time | 10 minutes

Cook Time | 10 minutes

Makes | 4 to 6 tortillas

Believe it or not, this recipe comes together with just five ingredients and added nutrients. It's a high-fiber alternative that's great for sandwich wraps, tacos, and pizza night!

½ cup (52 g) sifted coconut flour

3 tablespoons (12–15 g) psyllium husk fiber

1 tablespoon (8 g) tapioca flour

Pinch of kosher salt

1 cup (235 ml) nondairy milk, at room temperature

2–4 teaspoons (10–20 ml) olive oil

1. In a mixing bowl, whisk together the coconut flour, psyllium husk fiber, tapioca flour, and salt. There should be no flour clumps. Alternatively, use a blender to quickly pulse the ingredients together.
2. Gently stir the milk into the flour mixture. Once a dough ball forms, place it on a lightly floured (using tapioca flour) counter and knead the dough, pressing and stretching it, for 1 minute. Then form back into a dough ball, cover with plastic, and let sit for 10 to 15 minutes to expand in size.
3. Cut the dough into 4 even sections. Using a rolling pin, roll out each section between two pieces of wax paper, about ⅛ to ¼ inch (3 to 6 mm) thick. Then use a small saucepot lid to cut a circle in the dough. Repeat until you have 4 to 6 tortillas, each about 5 inches (13 cm) wide.
4. Heat a nonstick pan over medium-low heat. A 10- to 12-inch (25 to 30 cm) cast-iron frying or crepe pan works best. Brush the pan evenly with 2 teaspoons (10 ml) of the olive oil. Pick up the wax paper holding the rolled-out tortilla, carefully flip the paper over to place the tortilla into the hot pan, and peel off the wax paper carefully.
5. Cook for 2 to 3 minutes on each side until golden brown. If using a cast-iron pan, you will want to dry fry on low to medium-low heat for 1 to 2 minutes or less. They fry fast in cast-iron and the edges char quickly.

Storage
- Store the tortillas/flatbread in foil in the fridge for up to 2 weeks. Freeze cooled tortillas with wax paper between layers for up to 3 months.

6 { Meal Prep to Lunch Box

Perfect for kids and adults alike, these meal prep lunch options are easy to make ahead of time and are allergy-friendly for school. From pizza to patties, salads, and everything in between, there's something to fit all your needs.

Mexican Sweet Potato Patties, page 96

MEXICAN SWEET POTATO PATTIES

Gluten-free | Dairy-free Option | Vegetarian | Vegan Option | Nut-free | Egg-free

Prep Time | 20 minutes

Cook Time | 15 to 25 minutes

Makes | 6 to 8 patties

These patties are fun, lunch box–friendly, and so tasty your kids won't realize they're full of nutrients, too! They'll help meet everyone's dietary needs, and they are loaded with veggies, plant-based protein, vitamins, and fiber. Pair them with veggies and Avocado Ranch (page 46).

8–9 ounces (255–283 g) sweet potatoes, peeled, cooked, and mashed

¾–1 cup (139–185 g) cooked quinoa

2 tablespoons (32 g) tomato paste

⅓ cup (42 g) diced yellow onion

3 tablespoons (21 g) flax meal

1 teaspoon ground cumin

1 teaspoon garlic powder or 2 teaspoons (10 g) minced garlic

¼–½ teaspoon chili powder, to taste

¼ teaspoon kosher salt

¼ teaspoon black pepper

¼ cup (45 g) canned green chiles, drained

⅓ cup (40 g) gluten-free quick-cooking oats

1–2 tablespoons (5–10 g) grated Parmesan cheese or nutritional yeast (optional)

1. Line a sheet pan with parchment paper. In a food processor bowl or large mixing bowl, add the sweet potato, quinoa, tomato paste, onion, and flax meal. Mix until well combined. Mix in the spices and chiles. Add the oats and Parmesan (if using). Mix until combined.
2. Cover the bowl and place in the fridge for 10 to 20 minutes. Once chilled, form the mixture into 6 to 8 patties about 2½ inches (6 cm) wide and 1 inch (2.5 cm) thick. Place them on the prepared sheet pan.

To air fry:
1. Preheat the air fryer to 400°F (200°C). Once preheated, spray the basket with cooking spray. Place the patties in the air fryer basket, evenly spaced. Air fry for 11 to 12 minutes, flipping halfway through cooking.

To bake:
1. Preheat the oven to 400°F (200°C). Brush the tops of the patties with olive oil. Bake for 15 minutes. Gently flip the patties over and bake for 10 to 15 minutes longer, or until golden.

Notes
- Prepare the patty mixture and let it chill in the refrigerator, covered, overnight or for up to 2 days.
- For vegan and dairy-free patties, use nutritional yeast instead of Parmesan cheese.

Storage
- Store in an airtight container in the fridge for up to 7 days. Freeze cooled patties wrapped in wax paper in an airtight container for up to 3 months. To reheat, thaw frozen patties in the fridge overnight, and warm in the oven or air fry at 350°F (175°C) for 2 to 5 minutes.

CHICKEN SALAD TWO WAYS

Gluten-free | Grain-free | Dairy-free | Nut-free | Egg-free

Prep Time | 5 minutes

Chill Time | 10 to 15 minutes

Makes | 4 or 5 servings

This is my favorite recipe for picnics and packed lunches. It has everything you need! It's sweet, savory, creamy, crunchy, and completely dairy-free! Plus, it's high in protein and loaded with healthy fats. There are two variations so you can pick your favorite! Toss it with homemade Honey Mustard Dressing (page 47) for a sweet and zippy flavor, or keep it classic and creamy with Egg-Free Mayo (page 41). Pair this recipe with Cheesy Seedy Crackers (page 86).

3 cups (420 g) shredded cooked chicken

1 Granny Smith apple, cored, peeled, and chopped

½ cup (60 g) diced celery

1 tablespoon (4 g) chopped fresh dill or parsley

2 scallions, green portion, chopped

1–2 tablespoons (11–22 g) chopped dates

2 tablespoons (10 g) diced cooked nitrate-free bacon (optional)

½ teaspoon apple cider vinegar or lemon juice

¼ cup (60 ml) Honey Mustard Dressing (page 47) or Egg-Free Mayo (page 41)

Kosher salt and black pepper

1. In a large bowl, add the cooked chicken, apple, celery, dill, scallions, dates, bacon (if using), vinegar, and dressing. Mix together well. Season with salt and pepper.
2. Chill in the fridge for 10 to 15 minutes, then serve with Cheesy Seedy Crackers (page 86).

Note
- See page 167 for nitrate-free bacon suggestions.

Storage
- Store leftovers in an airtight container in the fridge for up to 5 days.

EASY ENGLISH MUFFIN PIZZA

Gluten-free | Dairy-free | Vegetarian |
Vegan | Nut-free | Egg-free

Prep Time | 5 minutes

Cook Time | 7 minutes

Makes | 2 pizzas

Using the Microwave English Muffins (page 88), I created a DIY pizza that satisfies your taste buds and nourishes you, too. Load it with all your favorite toppings, warm it up, and dig in!

1 doubled recipe Microwave
English Muffins (page 88)

TOPPINGS

Pizza sauce or Nomato Sauce (page 38)

Fresh-cut veggies

Uncured turkey pepperoni

Nondairy cheese

Chopped fresh basil

1. Preheat the oven to 350°F (175°C). Grease or line a baking sheet with parchment paper. Prepare the Microwave English Muffins.
2. After the muffins are toasted, add the toppings of choice. Place on the prepared baking sheet and bake for 7 to 8 minutes, or until the cheese is melted and the toppings are cooked. Remove from the oven and serve.

Note
- See page 167 for uncured turkey pepperoni suggestions and page 166 for nondairy cheese brand suggestions.

Storage
- Store leftovers in an airtight container in the fridge for up to 2 days.

AVOCADO RANCH TURKEY ROLL-UPS

Gluten-free | Dairy-free | Nut-free | Egg-free

Prep Time | 10 minutes

Makes | 1 serving

This classic is made with better-for-you ingredients for a bite-size lunch that's loaded with healthy fats, flavors, and veggies. Add your favorite fillings and serve them alongside peppers and Crispy Chickpeas (page 90) for a little extra crunch!

2 non-GMO corn tortillas

2 tablespoons (30 ml) Avocado Ranch (page 46)

2 ounces (57 g) gluten-free nitrate-free turkey lunch meat

¼ cup (30 g) sliced cucumber

¼ cup (37 g) sliced grape tomatoes (optional)

FOR SERVING

Mini bell peppers

Crispy Chickpeas (page 90)

1. Lay the corn tortillas on a counter or cutting board. Spread 1 tablespoon (15 ml) of the ranch evenly on each tortilla. Evenly distribute the lunch meat, cucumbers, and tomatoes on the tortillas.
2. Roll the tortillas up and over to form a wrap. Cut in half or leave whole. Serve alongside bell peppers and chickpeas for a complete meal.

Notes
- For a corn-free tortilla, swap in a gluten-free tortilla of choice.
- See page 167 for gluten-free nitrate-free turkey lunch meat suggestions and page 166 for gluten-free tortilla recommendations.

Storage
- Keep leftovers in an airtight container in the fridge for up to 2 days.

"CHEESY" TOMATO SOUP WITH CRISPY CHICKPEAS

Gluten-free | Grain-free | Dairy-free |
Vegetarian | Vegan | Nut-free | Egg-free

Prep Time | 10 minutes

Cook Time | 35 minutes

Makes | 5 or 6 servings

This is not your typical tomato soup. It is bursting with warm spices and "cheesy" flavor thanks to nutritional yeast. Top it with crispy chickpeas for a comforting meal you'll want to eat again and again.

1 tablespoon (15 ml) extra-virgin olive oil

2 medium yellow onions, chopped

2–3 cloves garlic, minced

3 cups (705 ml) nondairy milk

4 cups (940 ml) vegetable broth

3 large carrots, peeled and chopped

2 cans (28 ounces, or 794 g, each) whole peeled tomatoes

2–3 teaspoons (10–15 g) kosher salt

2 teaspoons (4 g) nutmeg

1 teaspoon black pepper

2 teaspoons (5 g) ground cumin

½ cup (40 g) nutritional yeast

Crispy Chickpeas (page 90)

1. In a large pot, heat the oil over medium heat. Add the onions and cook for 3 to 4 minutes, or until translucent. Add the garlic and cook for 1 minute, or until fragrant.
2. Add the nondairy milk, broth, carrots, tomatoes, seasonings, and nutritional yeast. Stir together. Cover and simmer over medium-low heat for 30 minutes, or until the carrots are fork tender.
3. Blend with an immersion blender and pulse until smooth. Alternatively, when cool enough, carefully transfer the mixture to a high-speed blender and blend until smooth. Then transfer the blended mixture back to the pot.
4. Adjust the seasonings to taste. Simmer for 5 minutes. Serve warm topped with crispy chickpeas.

Storage
- Store leftovers in an airtight container in the fridge for up to 5 days.

SALMON SALAD-STUFFED MINI BELL PEPPERS

Gluten-free | Grain-free | Dairy-free |
Nut-free | Egg-free

Prep Time | 10 minutes

Makes | 1 serving

High-protein, low-carb, and completely egg- and dairy-free, these stuffed peppers are a go-to lunch recipe for those times when you need something quick and nutritious while still being delicious! Pair it with Cheesy Seedy Crackers (page 86) for a satisfying meal.

3–4 mini bell peppers

½ cup (68 g) boneless skinless pink salmon (precooked and flaked or canned and drained)

2–3 tablespoons (30–45 ml) Avocado Ranch (page 46), hummus, or Egg-Free Mayo (page 41)

1 teaspoon lemon juice

Smoked paprika or ground cumin

Garlic powder

Kosher salt and black pepper

Finely chopped fresh cilantro

Cheesy Seedy Crackers (page 86) or gluten-free crackers

1. Slice the peppers in half lengthwise. Scrape out the seeds and membranes. Set aside.
2. In a medium bowl, add the salmon, ranch, lemon juice, and spices to taste. Mix until well combined.
3. Spoon the salmon salad mixture into the prepared pepper halves. Garnish with cilantro and serve with crackers.

Note
- To prep ahead: Place the unused pepper halves and salmon salad in separate airtight containers. Place in the fridge until ready to prep.

Storage
- Store leftovers in an airtight container in the fridge for up to 4 days.

CREAMY TUSCAN PASTA OR PASTA SALAD

Gluten-free | Dairy-free | Vegan Option | Nut-free | Egg-free Option

Prep Time | 10 minutes

Cook Time | 15 minutes

Makes | 4 or 5 servings

This light, creamy pasta dish is my go-to for every occasion. The artichokes and hearts of palm pack a zippy punch, but the real star is the sauce! Mix and match your favorite veggies to make this dish your own!

PASTA

Kosher salt

1 box (12–14 ounces, or 340–397 g) gluten-free pasta

½ pint (150 g) cherry tomatoes

¼ cup (12 g) chopped fresh basil

½ cup (50 g) pitted black olives

½ red or yellow onion, sliced or diced

1 cup (300 g) artichoke hearts or hearts of palm, sliced/quartered

Pinch of red pepper flakes

CREAMY DAIRY-FREE SAUCE

1 cup (240 g) hummus or Egg-Free Mayo (page 41)

1 teaspoon minced garlic or ½ teaspoon garlic powder

½ teaspoon onion powder

1 teaspoon dried Italian seasoning

Kosher salt and black pepper

½ cup (120 ml) vegetable or low-sodium chicken broth

1–2 teaspoons (5–10 ml) lemon juice

½ cup (50 g) grated Parmesan cheese or nutritional yeast

Olive oil, as needed

1. To make the pasta: Bring a large pot of water to a rolling boil. Season with salt. Add the pasta and stir. Cook to al dente, 1 minute less than the suggested time on the package. Overcooking will result in mushy pasta.
2. Drain the pasta, reserving 1 to 2 tablespoons (15 to 30 ml) of the pasta water. Do not rinse the pasta. Set aside.
3. To make the sauce: In the same pot, over low heat, add the sauce ingredients and whisk until creamy. Add the pasta and the reserved pasta water. Toss to combine. If the pasta seems dry, stir in 1 tablespoon (15 ml) of olive oil.
4. Gently stir in the remaining pasta ingredients. Serve warm, or bring to room temperature for a pasta salad side dish.

Notes

- For a protein boost, add 1 cup (140–160 g) diced cooked chicken, chickpeas, cooked peeled shrimp, or canned drained tuna.
- Double the sauce, and keep extra for refreshing the pasta once it has been chilled.
- Chickpea or lentil pasta may be substituted. See page 167 for gluten-free pasta recommendations.

Storage

- Store leftovers in an airtight container in the fridge for up to 7 days. If serving as pasta salad, let the pasta come to room temperature, then toss it with extra olive oil or sauce.

Build a Perfect Lunch Jar

Whether you want something light, refreshing, comforting, or zippy, lunch jars are the perfect way to make a portable, filling meal. Add your favorite toppings and mix-ins to make them your own!

The key to preserving the fresh taste and texture of each ingredient is to keep wet ingredients wet and dry ingredients dry.

- Always place the wettest and densest ingredients at the bottom. Layering grains and proteins as the base will prevent them from seeping into other ingredients or crushing them.
- Add a slice of lemon to keep the produce fresh. Then layer on the lightest, delicate ingredients to the top.
- Try 2-ounce (57 g) condiment cups for ingredients that are best stored separately until you are ready to eat (e.g., dry toppings, sauces, and seasonings).

ASIAN NOODLE JARS

Nut-free | Soy-free

Prep Time | 5 minutes

Makes | 1 or 2 servings

Better than takeout and healthier, too, these noodle jars are made with whole-food ingredients for a flavorful quick lunch. Enjoy on the go, at the office, or at home!

5 ounces (142 g) cooked rice noodles

2 ounces (57 g) lightly steamed or raw snow peas

⅓ cup (50 g) sliced bell pepper

2 ounces (57 g) diced cooked chicken

2 tablespoons (12 g) chopped scallion (green portion)

½ cup (35 g) shredded purple cabbage

1–2 lemon or lime slices

STORE SEPARATELY

1–2 tablespoons (15–30 ml) Soy-Free Stir-Fry Sauce (page 40) or gluten-free teriyaki sauce (optional)

2 tablespoons (30 ml) sesame oil (optional)

1. Layer the jars from heaviest to lightest with the citrus last to keep all of the ingredients fresh.
2. When ready to serve, add the sauce, extra seasonings, etc. Shake the jar, and then flip the contents into a bowl. Stir to combine.

Storage
- Store prepped jars (minus the sauce) in the fridge for up to 2 days.

CAESAR SALAD JARS WITH CHICKPEA "CROUTONS"

Dairy-free | Egg-free

Prep Time | 5 minutes

Makes | 1 or 2 servings

A light twist on a classic salad recipe! These meal prep salad jars are dairy-free, refreshing, and full of protein!

⅓ cup (62 g) cooked quinoa

⅓ cup (40 g) sliced vegetables (such as cucumber)

3 ounces (85 g) diced grilled chicken

1 cup (30 g) chopped romaine lettuce

Kosher salt and black pepper

1–2 lemon slices

STORE SEPARATELY

2 tablespoons (30 ml) Allergy-Friendly Caesar Dressing (page 45)

Crispy Chickpeas (page 90)

1. Layer the jars from heaviest to lightest with the lemon last to keep all of the ingredients fresh.
2. When ready to serve, add the dressing and crispy chickpeas, plus any additional seasonings. Shake the jar, and then flip the contents into a bowl.

Storage
- Store prepped jars (minus the dressing) in the fridge for up to 2 days.

EVERYTHING BUT THE KITCHEN SINK SOUP JARS

Dairy-free | Nut-free | Grain-free Option | Vegetarian Option

Prep Time | 5 to 10 minutes

Makes | 1 or 2 servings

Warm and flavorful with a refreshing zing, this soup jar recipe is a great way to use leftovers while also sneaking in veggies!

¾ cup (124 g) cooked rice or cauliflower rice

⅓ cup (75 g) canned diced tomatoes, drained

3 ounces (85 g) diced grilled chicken

½ cup (60 g) diced carrot

½ cup (55 g) diced celery

¼ cup (18 g) sliced mushrooms

STORE SEPARATELY

¼ teaspoon garlic powder

¼ teaspoon kosher salt

¼ teaspoon black pepper

¼ teaspoon Italian seasoning

¼ teaspoon red pepper flakes (optional)

¼ teaspoon onion powder

12–14 ounces (340–398 ml) vegetable or chicken broth

1 tablespoon (3 g) chopped fresh herbs (optional)

1. Layer the jars from heaviest to lightest with the mushrooms being last.
2. When ready to serve, add the seasonings and broth. Pour hot water (not boiling) into the jar or bowl, mix thoroughly, and let the ingredients sit for 1 to 2 minutes. Top with herbs (if using).

Storage
- Store prepped jars (with or without broth) in the fridge for up to 2 days.

MEZZA POWER LUNCH BOWL

Gluten-free | Dairy-free | Vegetarian |
Vegan | Nut-free | Egg-free

Prep Time | 10 minutes

Makes | 1 large or 2 small bowls

This refreshing Mediterranean-inspired recipe is easy to prep ahead of time and keeps fresh for multiple days. Keep this power bowl plant-based for a wholesome, filling vegan recipe, or bulk it up with your favorite protein!

DRESSING

1 tablespoon (15 ml) olive oil

2 teaspoons (10 ml) red wine vinegar
or lemon juice

½ teaspoon dried oregano

Kosher salt and black pepper

BOWL

1 cup (185 g) cooked quinoa

1 cup (30 g) fresh baby spinach

⅓ cup (40 g) sliced cucumber

¼ cup (30 g) sliced red onion or shallot

½ cup (75 g) sliced cherry tomatoes

½ cup (64 g) sliced black olives

3–4 fresh mint leaves (optional)

Lemon wedges (optional)

PROTEIN BOOSTERS (OPTIONAL)

3–4 tablespoons (30–40 g)
Crispy Chickpeas (page 90)

4 ounces (114 g) cooked chicken
breast or protein of choice

1. To make the dressing: In a small mixing bowl or glass jar, whisk together the olive oil, vinegar, and oregano. Season with salt and pepper.
2. To make the bowl: Arrange the quinoa and salad ingredients with protein boosters (if using) in a portable lunch container or a bowl. Drizzle the dressing on top and toss to combine. Garnish with the mint and lemon, if desired.

Storage
- Store leftovers in an airtight container in the fridge for up to 4 days.

7 Easy Prep Mains and Family Favorites

One of the most common complaints I hear when it comes to allergy-friendly cooking is that everything requires a million dishes and takes forever to make. Well, not anymore! Let me introduce you to a whole slew of sheet-pan, air fryer, and one-pot dinner recipes that are quick, comforting, and super adjustable to fit all your needs—so you can get out of the kitchen and back to the dinner table where you belong.

Sheet-Pan BBQ Salmon and Vegetable, page 119

SHEET-PAN COCONUT CRUST CHICKEN

Gluten-free | Grain-free | Dairy-free |
Nut-free | Egg-free

Prep Time | 15 minutes

Cook Time | 20 minutes

Makes | 4 or 5 servings

Kid-friendly chicken tenders with a nutrient-rich twist! This is everyone's favorite go-to meal. The coconut doesn't yield a strong flavor but makes this recipe grain-free, nut-free, and super crisp. Pair it with Hidden Veggie Mac and Cheese (page 138) for a dinner guaranteed to please.

⅓ cup (40 g) sifted coconut flour or Oat Flour (page 22)

½ cup (120 ml) nondairy milk or chicken broth

2 tablespoons (18 g) arrowroot starch or cornstarch

1 teaspoon garlic powder

1 teaspoon onion powder

½ teaspoon smoked paprika

½ teaspoon kosher salt

½ teaspoon black pepper

½ teaspoon ground cumin

¼ cup (32 g) flax meal

⅓ cup (28 g) shredded unsweetened coconut

1 pound (454 g) skinless chicken tenders

3 cups (390 g) sliced carrots or cauliflower florets

2 tablespoons (30 ml) olive oil

1. In one bowl, add the coconut flour. In a second bowl, whisk the milk and arrowroot starch. In a third bowl, add the garlic powder, onion powder, smoked paprika, salt, pepper, cumin, flax meal, and shredded coconut.
2. Dip each chicken tender into the flour mixture, coating evenly. Then dip into the milk mixture. Then place in the seasoning mixture, coating both sides evenly.

To bake:

1. Preheat the oven to 400°F (200°C). Line a sheet pan with parchment paper or foil. Place the coated chicken tenders in a single layer on the prepared sheet pan, arranging the carrots around the chicken. Drizzle the chicken and carrots with the olive oil. Bake for 20 to 22 minutes, or until golden brown on the outside and the internal temperature of the chicken reaches 165°F (74°C). Remove from the oven and serve.

To air fry:

1. Preheat the air fryer to 400°F (200°C). Spray the air fryer basket with a soy-free cooking spray. Once preheated, place half of the coated chicken tenders in the basket and spritz with olive oil spray. Arrange the carrots around the chicken (if there is room). Cook for 10 to 12 minutes, flipping halfway, or until the internal temperature of the chicken reaches 165°F (74°C). Remove the chicken and carrots, place on a clean plate, and cover them to keep warm. Repeat with the second batch of chicken and carrots.

Note
- To reheat, warm the tenders in the oven or air fryer to keep the breading crispy.

Storage
- Store leftovers in an airtight container in the fridge for up to 4 days.

SHEET-PAN BBQ PEACH SALMON AND VEGETABLES

Gluten-free | Dairy-free | Nut-free | Egg-free | Grain-free

Prep Time | 15 minutes

Cook Time | 22 minutes

Makes | 3 or 4 servings

A little sweet, a little spicy, and a whole lot of delicious, this is a complete dinner that requires minimal prep and cleanup!

SAUCE

⅓ cup (80 g) peach or apricot preserves

1½ teaspoons balsamic vinegar or apple cider vinegar

1 teaspoon grated fresh ginger or ½ teaspoon ground ginger

¼ teaspoon kosher salt

¼ teaspoon black pepper

¼ cup (60 ml) gluten-free barbecue sauce of choice

1 teaspoon chili powder

SALMON

3–4 boneless, skinless salmon fillets (6 ounces, or 168 g, each)

2–3 cups (175–275 g) green beans, broccoli florets, or sliced Brussels sprouts

1 large sweet potato, peeled and diced, or 2 cups (220 g) diced red potato

2 tablespoons (30 ml) olive oil

1 tablespoon (15 ml) lemon juice

Salt and black pepper

1–2 tablespoons (10–20 g) diced peaches, fresh or canned (optional)

1. To make the sauce: In a saucepan, whisk together all the sauce ingredients. Warm the sauce over medium heat for 2 to 3 minutes, stirring, until the flavors combine and thicken. Alternatively, place the ingredients in a microwave-safe bowl and microwave the sauce for 1 minute, stirring halfway through cooking. Taste and adjust the seasoning.
2. To make the salmon: Place the salmon fillets on a large plate or tray. Generously brush the sauce over each fillet. Place the salmon in the fridge while preparing the vegetables.
3. Preheat the oven to 400°F (200°C). Line a sheet pan with foil.
4. In a large bowl, toss the green beans and sweet potato in the oil and lemon juice, and generously season with salt and pepper. Spread the vegetables evenly on the prepared sheet pan. Bake for 10 minutes. Remove from the oven and toss the vegetables, moving them to one side of the pan. Place the fillets on the other side of the pan. Top each with the peaches (if using).
5. Bake for 10 minutes, or until the salmon has reached an internal temperature of 165°F (74°C). For extra crispy vegetables and a caramelized salmon topping, broil for the last 1 to 2 minutes at 500°F (260°C).
6. Remove from the oven and let the salmon rest for 5 minutes before serving.

Note
- You can prep the sauce up to 2 days ahead of time.

Storage
- Store leftovers in an airtight container in the fridge for up to 3 days.

SHEET-PAN CAULIFLOWER TACOS

Gluten-free | Grain-free | Dairy-free | Vegetarian | Nut-free | Egg-free

Prep Time | 5 to 8 minutes

Cook Time | 35 minutes

Makes | 3 or 4 servings

This is a family favorite: cauliflower is coated with a zesty tomato sauce and roasted to perfection for a vegan dinner that will have even the pickiest of eaters drooling!

¼ cup (62 g) tomato sauce

2 tablespoons (40 g) honey

¼ teaspoon garlic powder

½ teaspoon apple cider vinegar

½ teaspoon smoked paprika

½ teaspoon ground cumin

Pinch of cayenne or chili powder (optional)

¼ teaspoon salt

¼ cup (60 ml) olive oil

1 large head cauliflower, cut into small florets

Kosher salt and black pepper

Coconut Flour Tortilla/Flatbread (page 92) or gluten-free tortillas

GARNISHES (OPTIONAL)

Chopped scallion

Pico de gallo

Chopped fresh cilantro

Lime juice

Dairy-Free Sour Cream (page 36)

Diced jalapeño

1. Preheat the oven to 425°F (220°C). Line a large sheet pan with foil.
2. In a large bowl, mix the tomato sauce, honey, garlic powder, apple cider vinegar, paprika, cumin, cayenne (if using), salt, and oil. Add the cauliflower and toss to coat evenly. Spread the florets on the prepared pan, avoiding any overlap to ensure even cooking and crispy edges. Roast for 35 to 40 minutes, tossing once halfway through, until tender and charred on the edges. Season with salt and pepper.
3. To assemble, warm the gluten-free tortillas in the microwave or in the oven for easy rolling. Add the desired amount of roasted cauliflower to each tortilla and top with the optional garnishes.

Storage
- Store leftover roasted cauliflower in an airtight container in the fridge for up to 5 days.

THE GLUTEN-FREE FAMILY COOKBOOK

CAST-IRON SOCCA PIZZA (CUSTOMIZABLE)

Gluten-free | Grain-free | Dairy-free |
Vegetarian | Vegan | Nut-free | Egg-free

Prep Time | 20 minutes

Cook Time | 20 minutes

Makes | 2 or 3 servings

Pizza night just got better with this flatbread pizza recipe! Naturally high in protein thanks to the chickpea flour, it's grain-free, gluten-free, and ready in less than forty-five minutes. Have the kids load up all their favorite toppings, pop it in the oven, and dinner will be ready in no time! Pair this recipe with the Nomato Sauce (page 38) or Avocado Ranch (page 46).

SOCCA CRUST

1¼ cups (150 g) chickpea flour

3 tablespoons (45 ml) olive oil or avocado oil, divided

1¼ cups (295 ml) warm water

¼ teaspoon kosher salt

¼ teaspoon pepper

¼ teaspoon garlic powder (optional)

1 teaspoon dried herbs or seasonings of choice (optional)

TOPPINGS

Pizza sauce, tomato sauce, or Nomato Sauce (page 38)

Fresh-cut veggies of choice

Nondairy shredded cheese

Chopped fresh basil

Kosher salt and black pepper

PROTEIN CHOICES

Uncured turkey pepperoni

Cooked, diced chicken

Cooked, sliced sausage

1. To make the crust: In a bowl, whisk together the chickpea flour, 2 tablespoons (30 ml) of the olive oil, water, salt, pepper, garlic powder (if using), and seasonings of choice (if using). Let the mixture sit at room temperature for 15 to 20 minutes.
2. Preheat the broiler to 450°F (230°C) and place a 10- or 12-inch (25 or 30 cm) cast-iron or ovenproof skillet on the center rack (about 8 inches [20 cm] from the heat) for 10 minutes. (Use a wider skillet for a thinner crust.)
3. In the meantime, prepare the toppings.
4. Using oven mitts, carefully remove the skillet from the oven. Turn the oven to 425°F (220°C). Pour the remaining 1 tablespoon (15 ml) of oil into the hot skillet and evenly coat the bottom of the pan. Pour in the batter.
5. Bake for 5 to 8 minutes, or until the batter has set, checking after 5 minutes. Remove from the oven and add the toppings of choice. Return the skillet to the oven for 10 to 15 minutes, or until the cheese has melted and the crust is crisp. Check at 10 minutes for doneness.
6. Top with the basil and season with salt and pepper. Let cool for 2 to 3 minutes. Slice and serve.

Notes
- Prepare the crust ahead of time. Wrap the baked and fully cooled crust with foil and freeze for up to 3 months.
- See page 166 for nondairy cheese suggestions and page 167 for turkey pepperoni suggestions.

Storage
- Store leftovers in an airtight container in the fridge for 3 to 4 days.

CHICKEN AND WAFFLES

Gluten-free | Dairy-free | Egg-free | Nut-free Option

Prep Time | 15 minutes

Chill Time | 4 hours

Cook Time | 15 minutes

Makes | 4 servings

This is a healthier version of a Southern classic. Boneless, skinless chicken thighs are coated with a gluten-free breading and air fried or baked for a crispy crunch. Paired with Potato Waffles (page 65), it's a comfort food dinner you can feel good about! Serve this with Avocado Ranch (page 64).

CHICKEN

1½–2 pounds (680–910 g) skinless, boneless chicken thighs

¾ cup (180 ml) nondairy milk

1 teaspoon apple cider vinegar or lemon juice

½ teaspoon kosher salt

½ teaspoon garlic powder

¼ teaspoon smoked paprika

FLOUR COATING

⅓–½ cup (40–60 g) gluten-free all-purpose flour or Oat Flour (page 22)

½ teaspoon kosher salt

½ teaspoon black pepper

SEASONED PANKO

¼ teaspoon kosher salt

¼ teaspoon black pepper

½ teaspoon garlic powder

½ teaspoon onion powder

½ teaspoon smoked paprika

2 cups (70 g) sea salt potato chips or pork rinds, crushed

Potato Waffles (page 64)

1. To make the chicken: Place the chicken in a large bag or bowl. In a measuring cup, whisk the milk, vinegar, salt, garlic powder, and smoked paprika. Pour over the chicken. If using a bag, seal tightly and massage the chicken until it is evenly coated with the marinade. Refrigerate for at least 4 hours or up to 24 hours.
2. When ready to cook, drain the chicken, reserving the marinade in a wide bowl.
3. To make the flour coating: In a wide, flat bowl or rimmed plate, combine the flour, salt, and pepper. Whisk until no clumps remain.
4. To make the seasoned panko: In another wide bowl, combine the seasoned panko ingredients. Whisk until well blended.
5. Dredge each chicken thigh in the flour mixture until fully coated. Dip the thighs in the remaining marinade mixture, then in the panko. Set the coated chicken on a plate.

To air fry:
1. Preheat the air fryer to 400°F (200°C). Spray the air fryer basket with cooking spray. Working in batches, place the chicken in the air fryer basket and cook for 12 to 15 minutes (flipping halfway) or until the internal temperature reaches 165°F (74°C). Let rest for 5 minutes before serving with the potato waffles.

To bake:
1. Preheat the oven to 400°F (200°C). Line a sheet pan with parchment or foil. Place the coated chicken on the prepared sheet pan and place on the center rack. Bake for 18 to 25 minutes, or until the internal temperature reaches 165°F (74°C). Flip the chicken halfway for even baking. Let rest for 5 minutes before serving with the potato waffles.

Notes
- If using oat flour, do not flip the chicken at the halfway point to prevent the breading from falling off.
- See page 166 for gluten-free all-purpose flour suggestions.

Storage
- Store leftover chicken in an airtight container in the fridge for up to 4 days. Reheat in the air fryer or oven to crisp the breading.

TUNA PATTIES

Gluten-free | Dairy-free | Nut-free |
Egg-free

Prep Time | 10 minutes

Cook Time | 15 minutes

Makes | 6 to 8 servings

These are loaded with omega-3 fatty acids and hidden veggies for a healthy grab-and-go dinner your kids will be excited to eat. Pair this recipe with the Avocado Ranch (page 46) or Nomato Sauce (page 38).

2 cans (5 ounces, or 140 g, each) tuna in water, drained

1 teaspoon minced garlic or ½ teaspoon garlic powder

⅓ cup (43 g) diced yellow onion

⅓ cup (10 g) chopped spinach

½ teaspoon regular or smoked paprika

1 teaspoon cayenne pepper (optional)

½ teaspoon kosher salt or sea salt

¼ teaspoon black pepper

3 tablespoons (24 g) Oat Flour (page 22)

1 teaspoon Dijon mustard

2 flax eggs (see Notes) or 2 large eggs

3 tablespoons (12 g) chopped fresh parsley or ½ teaspoon dried

1. In a large mixing bowl, add the tuna, garlic, onion, spinach, spices, and oat flour. Mix to combine. Add the Dijon and flax eggs to the mixture and stir to combine. Fold in the parsley.
2. Using a large spoon or an ice cream scoop, scoop the mixture into equal-size balls (6 to 8 balls) and place on a sheet pan. Shape into patties ½ to 1 inch (1 to 2.5 cm) thick and about 3 inches (7.5 cm) wide. Chill the patties in the fridge for 15 to 20 minutes.

To air fry:

1. Preheat the air fryer to 400°F (200°C). Spray the air fryer basket with cooking spray. Add half the patties to the air fryer basket and cook for 12 to 14 minutes, flipping halfway through. Remove the cooked patties and repeat with the second batch.

To bake:

1. Preheat the oven to 400°F (200°C). Place the patties on a parchment-lined sheet pan and bake for 20 to 25 minutes, or until they are golden brown, flipping them halfway through cooking. Remove from the oven and let the patties cool completely.

Notes

- Use sustainable wild-caught canned tuna if possible. Make sure the tuna is packed in water and not vegetable oil. If the tuna mixture is too moist to hold the patty shape, add 1 tablespoon (8 g) of oat flour, then chill the mixture for 30 minutes.
- For flax eggs: Mix 2 tablespoons (14 g) flax meal with 6 tablespoons (90 ml) water in a small bowl, stir, and let sit for 5 minutes to thicken. Makes 2.

Storage

- Store leftovers in an airtight container in the fridge for up to 4 days. Freeze cooked or uncooked patties by wrapping them individually and freezing for up to 3 months. Place frozen patties in the fridge overnight before air frying or reheating.

THE GLUTEN-FREE FAMILY COOKBOOK

BAKED ITALIAN TURKEY MEATBALLS

Gluten-free | Grain-free | Dairy-free |
Nut-free Option | Egg-free

Prep Time | 15 minutes

Cook Time | 22 minutes

Makes | 4 or 5 servings

These are perfectly poppable on their own or super tasty paired with gluten-free noodles and your favorite sauce. And the meatballs are secretly full of veggies, but all you'll taste is the abundance of spice! Pair this recipe with Nomato Sauce (page 38) or Allergy-Friendly Caesar Dressing (page 45).

1 pound (454 g) ground turkey

2 teaspoons (6 g) minced garlic

2 teaspoons (2 g) Italian seasoning

1 teaspoon onion powder

⅛ teaspoon smoked paprika

¼ teaspoon kosher salt

¼ teaspoon black pepper

4 fresh basil leaves

1 large carrot, peeled and sliced

1 cup (30 g) packed fresh baby spinach

1–1½ tablespoons (16–24 g) tomato paste

¼ cup (20 g) gluten-free quick-cooking oats or 3 tablespoons (24 g) Almond Flour (page 25)

1. In a large bowl, add the turkey, garlic, Italian seasoning, onion powder, smoked paprika, salt, and pepper. Mix together well.
2. Place the basil, carrot, and spinach in a food processor bowl. Process until a panko bread crumb–like texture forms. Add the carrot mixture, tomato paste, and oats to the turkey mixture. Mix well. Form into golf-ball-size balls to make 15 to 18 meatballs.

To air fry:
1. Preheat the air fryer to 400°F (200°C). Spray the air fryer basket with cooking spray. Once preheated, place half of the meatballs in the basket and cook for 10 to 12 minutes, flipping halfway. Remove the meatballs, place on a clean plate, and cover them to keep warm. Repeat until all the meatballs are cooked.

To bake:
1. Preheat the oven to 400°F (200°C). Line a sheet pan with parchment paper or foil. Place the meatballs on the prepared baking sheet. Bake for 12 minutes, gently flip, and bake for 10 to 12 minutes. Broil for 2 minutes for a crispy exterior.

Notes
- If using a lean ground turkey, use the gluten-free quick-cooking oats option and not the almond flour to ensure moist meatballs.
- For a nut-free option, use the gluten-free quick-cooking oats.
- If not using a food processor, simply chop the vegetables finely.

Storage
- Store leftovers in an airtight container in the fridge for up to 4 days, or freeze for up to 3 months.

ONE-PAN CREAMY MUSTARD BAKED PORK CHOPS

Gluten-free | Grain-free | Dairy-free | Nut-free | Egg-free

Prep Time | 35 minutes

Cook Time | 15 minutes

Makes | 4 servings

Lock in the tangy flavor of my favorite mustard sauce and create the most tender, juicy pork chops of your dreams! Combined with roasted green beans, this dish will make a complete dinner that is on the table in less than an hour. Pair this recipe with Potato Waffles (page 64).

MARINADE

¼ cup (60 g) Dijon mustard

3–4 tablespoons (60–80 g) honey

1 teaspoon onion powder

¼–½ teaspoon sweet paprika or smoked paprika (optional)

1 teaspoon lemon juice

¼ cup (60 ml) olive oil, plus more as needed

Kosher salt and black pepper

Chopped fresh parsley (optional)

PORK CHOPS

4 boneless pork chops, each 1¼ to 1½ inches (3 to 4 cm) thick

1 tablespoon (15 ml) olive oil

GREEN BEANS

1 pound (454 g) fresh green beans, trimmed

1 tablespoon (15 ml) olive oil

½ teaspoon kosher salt

¼ teaspoon black pepper

Splash of lemon juice

1. To make the marinade: In a large bowl, combine the marinade ingredients. Reserve ¼ cup (60 ml) for basting and serving.
2. To make the pork chops: Add the pork chops to a bag or bowl. Add the marinade, tossing to coat. Cover and place in the fridge for 30 minutes and up to 24 hours.
3. When the pork chops are almost done marinating, preheat the oven to 400°F (200°C). Line a sheet pan with parchment paper or foil.
4. To make the green beans: Place the green beans in a large bowl along with the oil, salt, and pepper. Toss to evenly coat, then spread evenly onto one side of the prepared sheet pan.
5. In a skillet over medium-high heat, heat the oil. Remove the pork chops from the marinade, discarding the marinade, and place in the hot skillet; cook for 2 to 3 minutes on each side to sear. Place the seared pork chops on the sheet pan opposite the green beans. Brush a generous amount of the reserved marinade on top.
6. Bake for 15 to 20 minutes, flipping the pork chops halfway through baking and basting as needed, until the pork reaches an internal temperature of 145°F (63°C) and the green beans are tender. The pork may take longer to bake if you have extra-thick chops.
7. Transfer the pork to a plate and brush with the reserved marinade. Let rest for 5 minutes before serving. Season with salt and pepper, and garnish with parsley. Squeeze lemon juice over the green beans.

Storage
- Store leftovers in an airtight container in the fridge for up to 4 days.

SLOW COOKER GLUTEN-FREE SPAGHETTI

Gluten-free | Dairy-free | Vegetarian
Option | Vegan Option | Nut-free |
Egg-free

Prep Time | 5 to 10 minutes

Cook Time | 1 to 2+ hours

Makes | 5 or 6 servings

Make weeknights easy with this slow cooker spaghetti! A super hands-off meal, it features soft, gluten-free noodles, hidden veggies, and comforting tomato sauce. Add your favorite meat, or keep it vegetarian!

1 tablespoon (15 ml) olive oil

½ onion, finely diced

1 tablespoon (10 g) minced garlic

1 package (8 ounces, or 226 g) fresh sliced mushrooms

½ teaspoon kosher salt

½ cup (60 g) diced zucchini, green bell pepper, or vegetable of choice (optional)

1 jar (24 ounces, or 680 g) tomato basil spaghetti sauce

1 cup (235 ml) water

¼ cup (60 ml) low-sodium chicken or vegetable broth

1 box (12 ounces, or 340 g) dry gluten-free spaghetti noodles

½ cup (40 g) nutritional yeast or grated Parmesan cheese

1 can (24 ounces, or 680 g) tomato purée

Chopped fresh parsley or basil

Crushed red pepper flakes (optional)

1 pound (454 g) meat such as sausage, ground beef, or turkey (optional, see Notes)

1. In a large skillet over medium-high heat, heat the oil. Add the onions and garlic and cook for 2 to 3 minutes, until fragrant. Add the mushrooms and salt. Cook over medium heat for 3 minutes, until the mushrooms sweat and soften, scraping the bottom of the pan to release caramelized bits as it cooks. Stir in the diced vegetables (if using).

2. To the slow cooker, add the sauce, water, and broth. Stir to combine. Break the spaghetti noodles in half, and place them on top of the sauce. Make sure the noodles are layered in alternating directions. Add the vegetable mixture to the slow cooker and stir to combine. Sprinkle in the nutritional yeast, then pour the tomato purée on top.

3. Cover the slow cooker and cook on high for 1 to 2 hours or on low for up to 2½ hours, stirring periodically (if possible). Once the cook time is done and the noodles are soft, toss all the ingredients and serve. Garnish with fresh basil and crushed red pepper (if using).

Notes

- If using the meat add-in, brown it in a skillet before adding it to the slow cooker.
- Whole-grain and brown rice pasta take slightly longer to cook. Be sure to keep an eye on your pasta, stirring regularly, the first time you make it so that you know how long it takes in your slow cooker. Corn-based pasta should be stirred frequently to prevent it from overcooking. Overcooked pasta will become mushy. Chickpea/lentil flour–based noodles will not hold well in a slow cooker.
- See page 167 for gluten-free pasta suggestions.

Storage

- Store leftovers in an airtight container in the fridge for up to 5 days.

ONE-POT SOY-FREE STIR-FRY

Gluten-free | Grain-free | Dairy-free | Egg-free | Nut-free

Prep Time | 15 minutes

Cook Time | 15 minutes

Makes | 3 or 4 servings

An easy "clean out the fridge" dinner, this stir-fry is a great way to use up any leftover veggies you have on hand. Mix and match all your favorite ingredients, and toss them together in one pan for a quick meal that's even tastier than takeout!

2 tablespoons (30 ml) avocado oil or olive oil, divided

1 pound (454 g) boneless, skinless chicken breast, cut into 1-inch (2.5 cm) cubes

Salt and black pepper

1 teaspoon minced garlic

3 cups (450 g) sliced fresh vegetables (such as snow peas, mushrooms, peppers) or 1 bag (16 ounces, or 454 g) frozen stir-fry veggies

1 teaspoon grated fresh ginger (optional)

¼–⅓ cup (60–80 ml) Soy-Free Stir-Fry Sauce (page 40)

GARNISHES

Toasted sesame oil

Sesame seeds

Chopped scallion

1. In a large deep skillet or wok, heat 1 tablespoon (15 ml) of the oil over medium-high heat for 2 minutes. Add the chicken (working in batches if needed) and generously season with salt and pepper. Cook the chicken for 5 to 6 minutes (turning pieces), or until cooked through. Remove from the skillet and place on a plate.
2. Lower the heat to medium. Add the remaining 1 tablespoon (15 ml) oil, garlic, and veggies. Cook for 3 to 4 minutes, stirring occasionally, until slightly tender. Add the ginger (if using) and cook for 1 minute.
3. Shake the sauce in a glass jar, then add to the skillet. Place the chicken back into the skillet and stir to evenly coat in the sauce. Cook for 1 minute, or until the sauce bubbles and thickens. Season to taste.
4. Garnish with a drizzle of toasted sesame oil and a sprinkle of sesame seeds and scallion.

Notes
- Substitute shrimp for chicken. Use medium, deveined, tail-off uncooked shrimp. Note that the shrimp will cook faster.
- Serve this with cooked white rice, steamed cauliflower rice, or quinoa for a complete meal.
- Make the sauce ahead of time and keep in the fridge for a quick dinner.

Storage
- Store leftovers in an airtight container in the fridge for up to 4 days.

CAULIFLOWER-POTATO SHEPHERD'S PIE

Gluten-free | Dairy-free | Nut-free | Egg-free

Prep Time | 30 to 35 minutes

Cook Time | 20 to 25 minutes

Makes | 6 servings

This is a lower-carb take on a classic comfort food recipe. It features a host of veggies, but all your kids will notice is the creamy topping and the flavor of the meat!

FILLING

1 pound (454 g) ground turkey sausage or ground turkey

⅔ cup (84 g) diced onion

1 teaspoon minced garlic

1 package (8 ounces, or 226 g) fresh sliced mushrooms

¼ cup (64 g) tomato paste

2 tablespoons (16 g) gluten-free all-purpose flour or Oat Flour (page 22)

1 tablespoon (20 g) molasses (optional)

1 tablespoon (15 ml) gluten-free tamari, or Worcestershire sauce

¼ teaspoon smoked paprika

½ teaspoon kosher salt

½ teaspoon black pepper

1 cup (235 ml) beef broth

1½ cups (225 g) frozen vegetables

TOPPING

1 pound (454 g) gold potatoes, peeled, quartered, and steamed

3 cups (396 g) cauliflower florets, steamed

2 tablespoons (30 ml) olive oil

6 tablespoons (90 ml) nondairy milk

½ teaspoon garlic powder

¼ teaspoon kosher salt

¼ teaspoon black pepper

2 teaspoons (1 g) dried oregano

Chopped fresh parsley (optional)

1. Preheat the oven to 375°F (190°C)
2. To make the filling: In a large oven-safe skillet or cast-iron pan over medium-high heat, cook the turkey for 5 to 6 minutes, breaking it into small pieces as it cooks. Once cooked through and no pink remains, remove the turkey from the pan, but keep the fat in the skillet. Add olive oil if needed. Add the onion, garlic, and mushrooms, and cook over medium-high heat for 3 to 4 minutes, or until the mushrooms begin to sweat and reduce.
3. Add the cooked turkey back to the skillet. Add the tomato paste, flour, molasses (if using), tamari, smoked paprika, salt, and pepper. Stir until the ingredients are well combined and no clumps of tomato paste remain.
4. Add the broth and vegetables. Stir, bring to a boil, then lower to a simmer. Cover and simmer for 5 minutes, stirring occasionally. Adjust the seasonings to taste.
5. To make the topping: Place the steamed potatoes and cauliflower in a blender or food processor. Add the oil, milk, garlic powder, salt, pepper, and dried oregano. Blend the ingredients until they are thick and well combined. Remove the mixture from the blender. Alternatively, use a bowl to mash and mix the potato and cauliflower along with the milk and spices.
6. Spread the meat mixture evenly in an oven-safe skillet or a 9 x 13-inch (23 x 33 cm) casserole dish. Spoon the mashed potatoes evenly on top of the meat. If the baking dish looks very full, place it on a rimmed sheet pan so the filling doesn't bubble over into the oven. Bake uncovered for 25 to 30 minutes.
7. Remove from the oven and let sit for 15 minutes before serving. Garnish with parsley (if using).

Notes
- To make ahead, prepare the potato and cauliflower mash and the turkey and mushroom mixture ahead of time, storing in separate containers in the fridge. When ready to bake, layer the ingredients and bake for 20 minutes. Be sure to reheat the two layers separately before combining them to ensure they spread evenly!
- See page 167 for gluten-free Worcestershire sauce suggestions, and page 166 for gluten-free all-purpose flour suggestions.

Storage
- Store leftovers in an airtight container in the fridge for up to 5 days. Freeze completely cooled shepherd's pie for up to 1 month.

HIDDEN VEGGIE MAC AND CHEESE

Gluten-free | Dairy-free | Vegetarian |
Nut-free | Egg-free

Prep Time | 15 minutes

Cook Time | 35 minutes

Makes | 6 or 7 servings

This is an oven-baked recipe that's bursting with veggies and nutritional yeast, but it tastes like real cheese! Creamy and comforting, it can be served on its own or with your favorite mains, such as Sheet-Pan Coconut Crust Chicken (page 118) or Baked Italian Turkey Meatballs (page 128).

12–14 ounces (336–392 g) uncooked gluten-free elbow pasta

3 tablespoons (45 ml) olive oil or soy-free vegan butter, divided

1 cup (235 ml) nondairy milk

¼ cup (60 ml) nondairy cream or canned coconut milk

1 teaspoon garlic powder or minced garlic

½ teaspoon ground mustard

¼ teaspoon paprika

½ teaspoon kosher salt

½ cup (120 ml) Homemade Vegan Cheese Sauce (page 30) or dairy-free cheese sauce

1¼ cups (150 g) shredded dairy-free cheese or ⅓–½ cup (25–40 g) nutritional yeast

1–2 cups (150–300 g) frozen veggies (peas or carrots work best), steamed

TOPPINGS (OPTIONAL)

Fresh cracked black pepper

Fresh basil

Hot sauce

1. In a large saucepan or stockpot, cook the pasta according to package directions slightly less than al dente, about 1 minute less than the recommended time. Strain, then place in a large bowl and toss with 2 tablespoons (30 ml) of the oil.
2. Preheat the oven to 325°F (165°C) and spray a 9 x 13 inch (23 x 33 cm) baking dish or 12-inch (30 cm) cast-iron pan with cooking spray.
3. In the same saucepan over medium-low heat, add the remaining 1 tablespoon (15 ml) oil, milk, cream, garlic powder, mustard, paprika, and salt. Stir together over medium heat and bring to a light-medium simmer.
4. Add the pasta to the milk mixture. Gently mix, then decrease the heat to a low simmer. Add the cheese sauce and shredded cheese. Gently stir over low heat until the cheese is melted and the noodles are coated. A low heat is required for even melting.
5. Transfer the pasta to the prepared baking dish and add the steamed vegetables. Stir gently to combine. Bake for 20 to 25 minutes, or until the edges have browned and are crispy. Broil at the end for a few minutes if desired. Serve immediately, sprinkled with the desired toppings.

Notes
- For optional additions, try sautéed onions, shredded chicken, or spinach.
- Brown rice, chickpea, or a rice flour blend of gluten-free pasta works best.
- See page 166 for vegan butter, dairy-free cheese, and cheese sauce suggestions and page 167 for gluten-free pasta suggestions.

Storage
- Store in an airtight container and refrigerate for up to 4 days. Freeze leftovers in an airtight container (preferably the original baking dish); the texture and taste will vary. Reheat in the oven at 350°F (175°C). Add cheese sauce or nondairy milk if needed to loosen.

ITALIAN SPAGHETTI SQUASH CASSEROLE

Gluten-free | Grain-free | Dairy-free |
Vegetarian | Vegan | Nut-free | Egg-free

Prep Time | 25 minutes

Cook Time | 55 minutes

Makes | 4 or 5 servings

This dish is so warm and full of flavor. It's lightened-up comfort food that tastes so good no one will know it's actually good for you, too! Bake it all in a single dish for an easy dinner that is perfect for meal prep.

1 large spaghetti squash

2 tablespoons (30 ml) olive oil, divided

½ cup (64 g) diced onion

1–2 teaspoons (3–6 g) minced garlic

½ cup (75 g) diced red or green bell pepper

8 ounces (227 g) precooked Italian chicken sausage

Kosher salt and black pepper

½ cup (120 ml) thick marinara sauce

⅓ cup (80 ml) Dairy-Free Sour Cream (page 36) or nondairy yogurt

1 teaspoon dried Italian seasoning

Red pepper flakes (optional)

Nondairy cheese (optional)

Chopped fresh parsley or basil

1. Preheat the oven to 400°F (200°C). Line a sheet pan with foil.
2. Slice the squash in half lengthwise, scoop out the seeds, and drizzle with 1 tablespoon (15 ml) of the olive oil. Place each half cut-side down on the prepared sheet pan. Roast for 30 to 40 minutes, or until fork tender. Let cool, then use a fork to scrape the strands from the sides of the squash into a large bowl. Press the squash with paper towels to remove any excess moisture.
3. Lower the oven temperature to 350°F (175°C).
4. Place a large oven-safe skillet or cast-iron skillet over medium-high heat. Add the remaining 1 tablespoon (15 ml) oil, swirling to coat the skillet. Add the onion, garlic, bell pepper, sausage, salt, and pepper. Stir and cook for 5 to 7 minutes, or until the sausage is browned. Pour in the sauce, sour cream, Italian seasoning, and red pepper flakes (if using). Stir to combine.
5. Gently fold in the spaghetti squash strands, coating them evenly with the sauce. Simmer for 5 minutes to let the flavors combine and allow the liquid to reduce.
6. Top with cheese (if using). Transfer the skillet to the oven. Bake uncovered for 20 to 25 minutes, or until golden brown and bubbly on top. For an extra golden brown top, place the casserole under the broiler for 1 to 2 minutes.
7. Remove the dish from the oven and sprinkle with parsley. Let it rest for 5 minutes before serving.

Note
- See page 166 for nondairy cheese suggestions and page 167 for gluten-free sausage suggestions.

Storage
- Store leftovers in an airtight container in the fridge for up to 4 days.

MEXICAN RICE CASSEROLE

Gluten-free | Dairy-free | Vegetarian
Option | Nut-free | Egg-free

Prep Time | 15 minutes

Cook Time | 36 minutes

Makes | 4 to 6 servings

Not your average casserole recipe, this Mexican-inspired version is lightened up and full of veggies! Serve it as a tasty side, or bulk it up with your favorite protein for a complete meal.

1 tablespoon (15 ml) olive oil or avocado oil

½ cup (64 g) diced onion

2 teaspoons (6 g) minced garlic

1 cup (150 g) diced red or yellow bell pepper

1 cup (120 g) diced zucchini

1 teaspoon ground cumin

1–1½ teaspoons chili powder or 1½ tablespoons (9 g) taco seasoning

¼ teaspoon kosher salt

¼ teaspoon black pepper

1 cup (235 ml) low-sodium chicken or vegetable broth

1 can (14 ounces, or 392 g) fire-roasted tomatoes, drained

1 can (4 ounces, or 113 g) chopped green chiles

¾ cup (146 g) uncooked medium-grain white rice

1 cup (113 g) cauliflower rice, frozen or fresh

TOPPINGS AND MIX-INS (OPTIONAL)

Homemade Vegan Cheese Sauce (page 30)

Nondairy shredded cheese

Chopped fresh cilantro

Sliced jalapeño

1. Preheat the oven to 375°F (190°C).
2. In a large oven-safe skillet or cast-iron pan over medium-high heat, heat the oil. Add the onions and garlic and cook for 2 to 3 minutes, or until browned. Add the bell pepper, zucchini, cumin, chili powder, salt, and pepper. Stir and cook for 3 to 4 minutes. Add the broth, bring to a boil, and boil for 1 minute, stirring occasionally.
3. Remove from the heat and add the tomatoes, green chiles, white rice, and cauliflower rice. Stir and cover with foil.
4. Bake for 30 to 40 minutes, or until the rice is tender. Remove from the oven. Garnish with the toppings and mix-ins (if using), then serve.

Notes
- For added protein options, use cooked ground beef or cooked diced chicken.
- See page 166 for nondairy shredded cheese suggestions and page 167 for taco seasoning suggestions.

Storage
- Store leftovers in an airtight container in the fridge for up to 3 days.

GREEN BEAN CHICKEN CASSEROLE

Gluten-free | Grain-free | Dairy-free |
Nut-free Option | Egg-free Option

Prep Time | 10 minutes

Cook Time | 45 minutes

Makes | 4 or 5 servings

Finally, a casserole that meets everyone's dietary needs and still tastes great! Just combine the ingredients with my homemade sauce, and you've got yourself a family-friendly meal perfect for holidays, potlucks, and everything in between.

12 ounces (340 g) fresh or frozen green beans, cut into 2-inch (5 cm) pieces

1 tablespoon (15 ml) olive oil

⅓ cup (42 g) diced yellow onion

8 ounces (227 g) fresh sliced mushrooms

2 cups (280 g) cooked, diced or shredded chicken breast

CASSEROLE SAUCE

⅔ cup (150 g) Egg-Free Mayo (page 41), or plain hummus

½ cup (120 ml) nondairy cream

½ cup (120 ml) low-sodium chicken broth

¼ teaspoon onion powder

½ teaspoon garlic powder

½ cup (40 g) nutritional yeast

¼ teaspoon kosher salt, or to taste

⅛ teaspoon paprika

Pinch of black pepper

2 tablespoons (18 g) arrowroot starch or cornstarch

2 tablespoons (30 ml) water

POTATO CHIP TOPPING

4 cups (140 g) gluten-free potato chips, gluten-free cornflakes, or pork rinds

½ teaspoon garlic powder

2 tablespoons (30 ml) avocado oil or soy-free vegan butter, melted

1. Preheat the oven to 350°F (175°C). Spray an 8 x 4-inch (20 x 10 cm) casserole dish or 10- to 12-inch (26 to 30 cm) cast-iron skillet with cooking spray.
2. If using fresh green beans, steam in a steamer basket in a medium or large saucepan for 5 to 7 minutes, or until tender. Discard the water from the pot. If using frozen, cook according to the package directions. Drain as much excess water from the beans as possible. This will prevent a soggy casserole!
3. Transfer the cooked green beans to the prepared baking dish, spreading evenly on the bottom of the dish.
4. In a saucepan or deep skillet over medium heat, add the oil, swirling to evenly coat the bottom. Add the onions and mushrooms. Cook for 5 minutes, or until the mushrooms start to turn golden brown and the onions are translucent, stirring occasionally. Layer the mushrooms and onions on top of the green beans.
5. To make the sauce: In the same saucepan, add all the sauce ingredients except the arrowroot and water. Whisk together and bring to a light boil. Combine the arrowroot with the water in a small bowl. When the sauce comes to a boil, decrease the heat to low and slowly pour in the slurry. Whisk quickly to avoid clumps. Remove from the heat. Continue stirring occasionally for 1 to 3 minutes, or until the sauce thickens.
6. Pour 1 cup (235 ml) of the sauce over the mixture in the casserole dish. Layer the cooked chicken on top, and pour the remaining sauce over the chicken.
7. To make the topping: Place the potato chips in a food processor (or crush by hand). Blend into a fine, panko-like texture. Transfer to a small bowl and mix in the garlic powder and oil. Spread the topping on the casserole. Bake for 25 to 30 minutes, or until the top is golden brown around the edges.

Notes

- To make ahead, prepare the casserole (minus the topping) and refrigerate it for up to 24 hours before baking as directed.
- See page 166 for soy-free vegan butter and naturally gluten-free potato chip/cereal suggestions.

Storage

- Store leftovers in an airtight container in the fridge for up to 5 days.

Simple Soups and Stews

If I'm being honest, I enjoy soup all year long. There's just something so comforting about a myriad of warm flavors combined in a bowl. Plus, they're an easy way to sneak in veggies, and the kids will never know! Quick and easy to make, the recipes in this chapter feature light and refreshing flavors and cozy soups that are so creamy you'd never guess they're dairy-free!

Quick Southwestern Beef Soup, page 150

CREAMY DAIRY-FREE MUSHROOM SOUP

Gluten-free | Dairy-free | Vegetarian |
Vegan | Nut-free

Prep Time | 15 minutes

Cook Time | 45 minutes

Makes | 3 or 4 servings

This mushroom soup is the best source of comfort on a cold winter day. It will warm you up from the outside in. Light and creamy, it's packed with nutrients and tastes even better paired with homemade crackers, salad, or a plant-based sandwich!

¼ cup (60 ml) naturally refined coconut oil, avocado oil, or soy-free vegan butter

1½ cups (240 g) chopped yellow onion

1 pound (454 g) cremini or white button mushrooms, sliced

⅓ cup (80 ml) dry white wine (optional)

2 teaspoons (2 g) dried dill or
1½ tablespoons (6 g) finely chopped fresh dill

2–4 teaspoons (5–10 g) smoked paprika

1 tablespoon (15 ml) gluten-free tamari or coconut aminos

2½ cups (570 ml) vegetable or low-sodium chicken broth

1 cup (235 ml) nondairy milk

3 tablespoons (27 g) arrowroot starch

1 teaspoon kosher salt

Black pepper

2 teaspoons (10 ml) lemon juice

¼ cup (15 g) chopped fresh parsley, plus extra for garnish

½ cup (120 ml) full-fat coconut milk, chilled to thicken

1. Heat a large pot over medium heat. Add the oil, swirling to coat the bottom of the pot. Add the onions and sauté for 5 minutes. Add the mushrooms and sauté for 5 minutes. Stir in the wine (if using), dill, paprika, tamari, and broth. Decrease the heat to low, cover, and simmer for 15 minutes.
2. In a separate small bowl, whisk the milk and arrowroot starch. Pour the mixture into the soup and stir thoroughly to blend. Cover the pot and simmer for 15 minutes, stirring occasionally.
3. Stir in the salt, black pepper, lemon juice, parsley, and solid coconut cream. Mix together, and allow to heat through over low heat, about 3 to 5 minutes. Do not boil.
4. Garnish with parsley and pepper. Serve immediately.

Notes
- Tapioca starch may be subbed for arrowroot starch, but the texture will vary.
- See page 166 for vegan butter suggestions and page 167 for coconut aminos suggestions.

Storage
- Store in an airtight container in the fridge for 3 to 4 days, or freeze for up to 3 months.

CREAMY ROASTED CAULIFLOWER TOSCANA

Gluten-free | Grain-free | Dairy-free |
Nut-free | Egg-free

Prep Time | 10 minutes

Cook Time | 45 minutes

Makes | 4 servings

Inspired by classic Toscana soup, my version is a cozy better-for-you comfort food that fills you up without weighing you down. Cauliflower and potatoes are roasted to bring out even more flavor, then blended together for the creamiest recipe that will have you dreaming about dinner for days!

1 pound (454 g) cauliflower florets

1¼ cups (135 g) baby potatoes, quartered

2 tablespoons (30 ml) olive oil, divided

¼ teaspoon kosher salt, plus more as needed

¼ teaspoon pepper, plus more as needed

½ teaspoon garlic powder

10 ounces (280 g) Italian sausage or chorizo, sliced or crumbled

3 pieces uncured nitrate-free turkey bacon, chopped

1 small yellow onion, diced

2 cloves garlic, minced

4 cups (940 ml) low-sodium chicken broth

1 cup (235 ml) full-fat or light coconut milk

3–4 cups (90–120 g) fresh baby spinach

1. Preheat the oven to 400°F (200°C). Line a sheet pan with parchment.
2. Place the cauliflower florets and potatoes on the prepared sheet pan. Drizzle with 1 tablespoon (15 ml) of the olive oil, then sprinkle with the salt, pepper, and garlic powder. Toss to coat, then spread out in a single layer. Bake for 25 minutes, or until fork tender.
3. In a large Dutch oven, heat the remaining 1 tablespoon (15 ml) olive oil over medium heat. Add the sausage and bacon and cook, stirring occasionally, until the sausage is browned and the bacon is crispy. Remove to a plate and set aside.
4. Drain all but 2 tablespoons (30 ml) of the grease from the Dutch oven. Add the onions and cook for 3 to 4 minutes, until soft. Add the garlic and cook for 30 seconds, stirring constantly. Add the roasted cauliflower, 1 cup (110 g) of the potatoes (reserving the rest), and the chicken broth. Season with salt and pepper. Bring to a light boil, then lower to a simmer for 5 minutes.
5. Use an immersion blender to purée the mixture in the saucepan. Alternatively, allow it to cool slightly, then carefully transfer the soup in batches to a blender to purée.
6. Add the coconut milk and bring to a gentle simmer for 5 minutes. Dice the reserved roasted potatoes. Add the remaining potatoes, sausage, bacon, and spinach. Simmer until the spinach is wilted, about 5 minutes. Season to taste.

Notes
- To remove excess grease (if desired), rinse cooked sausage in a strainer before adding back to the pot.
- See page 167 for turkey bacon and sausage suggestions.

Storage
- Store leftovers in an airtight container in the fridge for up to 5 days.

QUICK SOUTHWESTERN BEEF SOUP

Gluten-free | Grain-free | Dairy-free | Nut-free | Egg-free

Prep Time | 10 minutes

Cook Time | 10 to 15 minutes

Makes | 4 or 5 servings

Warm spices, light broth, and tender beef combine to create the easiest go-to soup. It comes together in minutes for a filling meal that couldn't be easier to make!

1 tablespoon (15 ml) olive oil

1 pound (454 g) lean beef stew meat, cubed

⅔ cup (110 g) chopped yellow onion

3 cloves garlic, minced

4–5 cups (1–1.2 L) low-sodium chicken broth

1 teaspoon ground cumin

¼ teaspoon chili powder

½ teaspoon black pepper

¼ teaspoon kosher salt, or to taste

2½ cups (275 g) peeled, diced sweet potatoes

1 can (10 ounces, or 280 g) diced tomatoes with green chiles, drained

1 tablespoon (15 ml) lime juice

1 avocado, peeled, pitted, and diced, divided

½ cup (8 g) chopped fresh cilantro

Lime wedges

1. Heat the oil in a large stockpot over medium-high heat. Add the cubed beef, working in batches if needed and adding more oil as needed. Cook for 2 to 3 minutes per side. Remove the browned beef from the pot and place in a bowl.
2. Add the onions and garlic to the pot and cook for about 3 minutes, or until the onions are translucent. Stir in the cooked beef, broth, cumin, chili powder, pepper, salt, and sweet potatoes. Bring to a boil; decrease the heat and simmer for 10 to 15 minutes, until the beef is tender. Remove from the heat and stir in the tomatoes, lime juice, and half of the avocado. Garnish with the remaining avocado and the cilantro and serve with lime wedges.

Note
- Use ground turkey or chicken instead of ground beef.

Storage
- Store leftovers in an airtight container in the fridge for up to 5 days.

SWEET POTATO "NO PEANUT" STEW

Gluten-free | Dairy-free | Vegetarian
Option | Nut-free Option

Prep Time | 20 minutes

Cook Time | 1 hour 10 minutes

Makes | 5 to 7 servings

This stew is the ultimate hearty winter meal. It can be made extra spicy or kept mild, loaded with beef or kept completely plant-based to fit your needs. No matter how you serve it, it'll have your family begging for seconds!

SAUCE

1 cup (245 g) tomato sauce or plain diced canned tomatoes

½ cup (130 g) Sunflower Seed Butter (page 42) or almond butter

2 teaspoons (5 g) smoked paprika, or to taste

½ teaspoon ground coriander

1 teaspoon cayenne pepper (optional)

½ teaspoon kosher salt

½ teaspoon black pepper

STEW

2 tablespoons (30 ml) olive oil, or avocado oil, divided

1 pound (454 g) diced stew meat (optional)

1 cup (160 g) chopped yellow onion

1 tablespoon (6 g) grated fresh ginger or 1 teaspoon ground ginger

1 teaspoon minced garlic (3 small cloves)

10 ounces (283 g) sweet potatoes, peeled and diced into 1-inch (2.5 cm) cubes

⅔ cup (87 g) peeled, sliced carrots (optional)

2 cups (475 ml) vegetable or low-sodium chicken broth (2½ cups [595 ml] if adding meat)

3 cups (90 g) fresh baby spinach

1. To make the sauce: Add all the sauce ingredients to a blender or food processor. Pulse to combine. Alternatively, place them in a large mixing bowl and whisk to combine. Set aside.
2. To make the stew: If using meat, heat a large, heavy-bottomed pot over medium-high heat. Add 1 tablespoon (15 ml) of the oil and swirl to coat the bottom of the pot. Add the meat (if using) and brown for 5 minutes, turning once. When the meat is almost cooked through, remove from the pot and place on a large plate or bowl. Set aside.
3. In the same pot, add the remaining 1 tablespoon (15 ml) oil and swirl to coat the bottom of the pot. Add the onions and sauté for 3 to 4 minutes, stirring often and scraping any browned bits off the bottom of the pot. Add the ginger and garlic. Sauté for 1 to 2 minutes. Add the sweet potatoes and carrots (if using). Stir to combine.
4. Stir in the sauce and broth. Simmer, covered, for 1 hour, or until the potatoes are tender and the meat is cooked through. Remove the lid and add the baby spinach. Let cook for 3 to 5 minutes to wilt the spinach.

Notes
- If you don't have ground coriander, use ¾ teaspoon ground cumin.
- In place of the stew meat, you may swap in boneless skinless chicken breast, a lean cut of beef, or pork loin.
- For vegetarian/vegan options, swap the meat out with chickpeas.

Storage
- Store in an airtight container in the fridge for 3 to 5 days, or freeze for up to 6 months.

30-MINUTE VEGETABLE CHICKEN CURRY SOUP

Gluten-free | Grain-free | Dairy-free |
Vegetarian Option | Nut-free | Egg-free

Prep Time | 10 minutes

Cook Time | 15 minutes

Makes | 4 servings

A high-protein, veggie-loaded meal that's ready in thirty minutes? Sign me up! This quick, kid-friendly curry puts all your leftovers to use in the most incredibly tasty soup.

2 cans (13.6 ounces, or 406 ml, each) full-fat or light coconut milk

2 cups (475 ml) low-sodium chicken or vegetable broth

3–4 tablespoons (48–64 g) red curry paste

1 tablespoon (6 g) grated fresh ginger

2 cups (280 g) shredded cooked chicken

2 cups (150 g) broccoli florets

1 cup (130 g) sliced carrots

1 red or green bell pepper, cored and sliced

I tablespoon (15 ml) gluten-free fish sauce or 1 teaspoon kosher salt

Juice of ½ lime

Thai basil (optional)

1. In a 3-quart (2.7 L) saucepan, add the coconut milk, broth, red curry paste, and ginger. Bring to a boil, then lower to medium heat. Stir in the chicken, broccoli, carrots, and bell pepper. Cook over medium heat for 10 to 12 minutes, or until the carrots are tender. Add the fish sauce and lime juice and stir to combine. Serve, garnished with Thai basil (if using).

Notes
- For a vegetarian option, omit the chicken and add more vegetables.
- See page 167 for gluten-free fish sauce recommendations.

Storage
- Store in an airtight container in the fridge for up to 5 days, or freeze for up to 3 months.

9 { Desserts

What's life without a little balance, am I right? We all deserve a sweet treat every once in a while—but options for those with food allergies can be hard to find. So I took some of my favorite childhood desserts and gave them an allergy-friendly makeover. In this chapter, you'll find classic desserts for every season and occasion that have all the flavor you love with none of the ingredients you don't.

Go-To Sugar Cookies, page 160

NO-BAKE CHOCOLATE CRUNCH COOKIES

Gluten-free | Grain-free Option |
Vegetarian | Vegan | Dairy-free |
Egg-free| Nut-free Option

Prep Time | 10 minutes

Cook Time | 15 minutes

Makes | 18 to 20 cookies

Think Little Debbie, but better! Inspired by the Star Crunch cookies of my childhood, this no-bake version is made with better-for-you ingredients for a dessert we can all love!

4 ounces (113 g) dairy-free dark chocolate

¾ cup (190 g) Sunflower Seed Butter (page 42), no-stir almond butter, or cashew butter

⅔ cup (230 g) honey or agave syrup

1 teaspoon pure vanilla extract (optional)

3 cups (240 g) unsweetened coconut flakes

1 cup (120 g) gluten-free granola or chopped nut/seed mix

Pinch of sea salt (optional)

1. Line a baking sheet with parchment paper. Place a large saucepan over medium-high heat. Add the dark chocolate, sunflower seed butter, and honey. Stir to combine. Bring the mixture to a boil, then remove from the heat and stir in the vanilla.
2. Working quickly, use a silicone spatula to gently stir in the coconut and granola until they are well coated.
3. Using a large spoon or an ice cream scoop, scoop out the batter into clusters and place them on the prepared baking sheet. Shape the cookies as quickly as possible. Once the mixture begins to cool, the batter will harden and be difficult to work with.
4. Sprinkle the cookies with sea salt, if desired. Place the cookies in the fridge for 15 to 20 minutes to chill and harden before removing them from the baking sheet.

Notes
- Be sure to use a smaller baking sheet so you can fit it in the fridge or freezer.
- If nuts are well tolerated, substitute the coconut flakes with slivered almonds for a healthy fat alternative that adds a bit of crunch!
- Milk chocolate may be substituted for dark chocolate, if dairy can be tolerated. Check the ingredient list of your preferred chocolate for gluten or soy. See page 166 for dairy-free dark chocolate suggestions.

Storage
- Store cookies in an airtight container in the fridge for up to 1 week, or freeze for up to 6 weeks.

NO-BAKE CHOCOLATE "PEANUT-FREE" PB PIE

Gluten-free | Dairy-free | Vegetarian |
Vegan | Nut-free | Egg-free

Prep Time | 1 hour

Cook Time | 20 minutes

Makes | 8 to 10 servings

One pie, two crust options, this no-bake recipe is always guaranteed to please. Made with sunflower seed butter or almond butter and coconut milk, it's completely peanut-, gluten-, and dairy-free for a decadent "PB" pie everyone can enjoy!

GLUTEN-FREE CHOCOLATE COOKIE CRUST

18–20 (250 g) gluten-free/vegan/nut-free chocolate cookies

3–4 tablespoons (45–60 ml) naturally refined coconut oil, melted

DATE CRUST (GRAIN-FREE AND REFINED SUGAR-FREE)

1½ cups (175 g) pitted dates

½ cup (40 g) gluten-free quick-cooking oats

⅓ cup (27 g) unsweetened cocoa powder

Pinch of sea salt

2–3 tablespoons (30–45 ml) naturally refined coconut oil, melted

FILLING

1 can (13.6 ounces, or 386 ml) coconut cream, chilled for 24 hours

2 cans (13.6 ounces, or 386 ml) full-fat coconut milk, chilled for 24 hours

¼ cup (20 g) unsweetened cocoa powder

½ cup (100 g) fine raw sugar2 tablespoons (30 ml) maple syrup

1 teaspoon pure vanilla extract

½ cup (130 g) Sunflower Seed Butter (page 42) or creamy no-stir almond butter

Dairy-free dark chocolate chips

1. To make the gluten-free chocolate cookie crust: Spray an 8-inch (20 cm) pie plate with cooking spray or line the bottom with parchment paper for easy slicing. Place the cookies in a food processor bowl or blender. Pulse until a crumb texture is formed. Add 3 tablespoons (45 ml) of the melted oil and pulse again until well combined. If the batter is too dry, add ½ to 1 tablespoon (8 to 15 ml) of melted oil and pulse again. Transfer the crust mixture to the prepared pie plate. Press the mixture evenly into the bottom and up the sides. Chill in the fridge for at least 30 minutes before adding the filling.

2. To make the date crust: Line an 8-inch (20 cm) pie pan with parchment paper for easy slicing. Place the dates, oats, cocoa powder, and pinch of salt in a food processor bowl or blender. Pulse until the batter is well combined and resembles a coarse sand texture. Add 1 tablespoon (15 ml) of the melted coconut oil and pulse again. The texture should be sticky. If it is crumbly and doesn't hold together when pinched between two fingers, add an additional 1 to 2 tablespoons (15 to 30 ml) melted coconut oil and pulse again to combine. Transfer the crust mixture to the prepared pie pan. Press the crust mixture evenly into the bottom and up the sides. Chill in the fridge for 30 to 45 minutes or in the freezer for 15 to 20 minutes.

3. To make the filling: Place the thickened portion of the chilled coconut cream and the thickened portion of the chilled coconut milk in a stand mixer bowl fitted with the paddle attachment or a mixing bowl. Discard the remaining liquid from the can or use in another recipe. Gently cream together until it is a thick, cream cheese–like texture. Add the cocoa powder, sugar, maple syrup, and vanilla. Beat on medium speed for 2 minutes, or until the batter is mixed thoroughly and is light in texture. Stir in the sunflower seed butter and gently mix until combined. If the batter is too thick, add a splash of nondairy milk.

4. Remove the pie crust from the fridge/freezer and pour in the filling. Using the back of a spoon, spread the filling evenly, almost to the top edge of the crust. Top with the chocolate chips.

5. Freeze for 20 minutes to make cutting easier, or place the pie in the refrigerator until ready to eat. Alternatively, freeze for at least 1 hour for more of an ice cream cake/frozen pie texture.

Notes
- If using the date crust, be sure to let it thaw on the counter for 30 minutes before slicing.
- See page 166 for gluten-free cookie, soy-free vegan butter, and dairy-free dark chocolate chip recommendations.

Storage
- Cover tightly with foil and store in the fridge for 3 to 5 days, or freeze for up to 3 months.

GO-TO SUGAR COOKIES

Gluten-free | Dairy-free | Vegetarian |
Vegan | Egg-free

Prep Time | 10 minutes

Chill Time | 30 minutes

Cook Time | 10 minutes

Makes | 12 to 15 cookies

This gluten-free cookie mix is a game-changing recipe! The mix is sweet and satisfying, and it can be wrapped up with a bow for a fun DIY gift. Use it on its own for gluten-free cookies or as a base for all your favorite desserts, such as fruit pizza and cookie bars.

1⅓–1⅔ cups (150 g) Oat Flour (page 22)

1 cup (112 g) Almond Flour (page 25)

1 teaspoon baking powder

Pinch of ground cinnamon (optional)

⅓ cup (80 ml) avocado oil or naturally refined coconut oil

½ cup (120 ml) maple syrup

¼ cup (50 g) sparkling cane sugar for rolling

1. Place the oat flour, almond flour, baking powder, cinnamon (if using), oil, and maple syrup in a mixing bowl. Beat with a hand mixer or in a stand mixer for 1 minute. Gather the dough into a ball and cover with plastic wrap. Place in the fridge to chill for 30 to 40 minutes, or until firm enough to roll.
2. While the dough chills, preheat the oven to 350°F (175°C). Line a baking sheet with parchment paper.
3. Remove the chilled dough from the fridge. Use a cookie dough scoop or spoon to shape the dough into 1-inch (2.5 cm) balls. Roll the cookie dough balls in the sparkling cane sugar, and place them on the prepared baking sheet 1 to 2 inches (2.5 to 5 cm) apart. Use a cookie stamp to create a fun design or leave as is.
4. Bake the cookies for 10 to 12 minutes. Remove from the oven and let the cookies cool completely before transferring from the baking sheet to a cooling rack.

Storage
- Store cooled cookies in an airtight container in the pantry for up to 4 days. To freeze the cookie dough, wrap in plastic wrap or a freezer-friendly bag and freeze for up to 3 months.

ALLERGY-FRIENDLY CUPCAKES (CHOCOLATE/VANILLA)

Gluten-free | Dairy-free | Vegan | Vegetarian | Nut-free | Egg-free

Prep Time | 10 minutes

Optional Rest Time | 10 minutes

Cook Time | 18 to 22 minutes

Makes | 9 or 10 cupcakes

Made with oat flour and baked to fluffy perfection, this recipe is your staple for gluten-free baking! Use it to make chocolate or vanilla cupcakes for parties, holidays, and everything in between.

1½ teaspoons apple cider vinegar

1 cup (235 ml) nondairy milk, at room temperature or slightly warmed

1½ cups (180 g) Oat Flour (page 22)

½ cup (40 g) unsweetened cocoa powder

½ cup (100 g) fine raw sugar (cane sugar) or sugar substitute

1 teaspoon baking soda

¼ teaspoon kosher salt

3 tablespoons (45 ml) naturally refined coconut oil or avocado oil or soy-free vegan butter, melted

2–3 tablespoons (30–45 ml) maple syrup or (40–60 g) honey

1 teaspoon pure vanilla extract

TOPPING

1 recipe Coconut Cream Frosting/Whipped Cream (page 32)

1. Preheat the oven to 350°F (175°C). Line a 12-count muffin pan with paper liners.
2. In a small bowl, combine the apple cider vinegar and milk. Stir and let stand for a full 5 minutes to curdle.
3. In a large bowl, whisk together the oat flour, cocoa powder, sugar, baking soda, and salt.
4. If using coconut oil or butter, gently warm the milk mixture for about 30 to 45 seconds in the microwave. Skip this step if using oil.
5. Combine the oil of choice, maple syrup, and vanilla with the milk mixture. Working in batches, pour the wet ingredients into the dry ingredients, and stir until they are just combined. For more rise and consistent texture, let the batter sit at room temperature for 10 to 15 minutes before pouring into the muffin pan.
6. Spoon the batter into 9 or 10 cups in the prepared muffin pan, filling them three-quarters full. Bake for 18 to 22 minutes, or until a toothpick inserted into the center of a cupcake comes out clean. Remove from the oven, set the muffin pan on a wire rack, and let cool for 5 to 10 minutes. Remove the cupcakes from the pan to continue to cool.
7. Once completely cooled, decorate with frosting.

Notes
- To create fluffy swirls of frosting, use a pastry bag with a star tip. For a touch of glitter, sprinkle some raw sugar on top.
- See page 166 for soy-free vegan butter and sugar substitute suggestions.
- To make a vanilla option: Replace the ½ cup (40 g) cocoa powder with ⅓ cup (40 g) more oat flour or almond flour. Add an extra ½ teaspoon of pure vanilla extract.

Storage
- Store leftovers in an airtight container in the fridge for up to 5 days.

FRUIT PIZZA WITH COCONUT WHIPPED CREAM

Gluten-free | Dairy-free | Vegetarian |
Vegan | Nut-free | Egg-free

Prep Time | 40 minutes

Cook Time | 16 minutes

Makes | 4 or 5 servings

This is a fun dessert the kids will love to decorate themselves. Gluten-free dough forms a sweet, crisp base and is topped with my Coconut Cream Frosting/ Whipped Cream (page 32) and all the colorful fixin's!

CRUST

1⅓–1⅔ cups (150 g) Oat Flour (page 22)

1 cup (112 g) Almond Flour (page 25)

1 teaspoon baking powder

⅓ cup (80 ml) naturally refined coconut oil or avocado oil

½ cup (120 ml) maple syrup

TOPPINGS

Coconut Cream Frosting/
Whipped Cream (page 32)

Fruit of choice, such as kiwi, strawberries, or blueberries

Dairy-free chocolate chips

1. Preheat the oven to 350°F (175°C). Grease an 8- or 10-inch (20 or 25 cm) cast-iron pan.
2. To make the crust: Place the oat flour, almond flour, baking powder, oil, and maple syrup in a mixing bowl and beat with a hand mixer or in a stand mixer for 1 minute. Roll the dough into a ball, cover with plastic wrap, and place in the fridge for 30 minutes to chill.
3. Remove the plastic wrap and place the chilled dough ball on a well-floured surface or wax paper sprinkled with oat flour. Place the plastic wrap on top of the dough. Using a rolling pin, roll the dough into an 8- to 10-inch (20 to 25 cm) circle about ½ inch (1 cm) thick. Gather the remaining dough into a ball and repeat for 2 crusts, if desired. See Notes for leftover dough.
4. Place the rolled-out dough in the greased cast-iron pan and evenly flatten to the bottom of the pan. Run a spatula around the edges of the pan so it is easier to remove after baking.
5. Bake for 16 to 20 minutes, or until light golden on the edges.
6. Let the crust cool completely, then remove from the pan and place on a plate or serving tray. Spread the frosting on top and add your toppings of choice. Refrigerate for 15 to 20 minutes, then enjoy.

Notes
- If there is leftover dough, roll it out for a second crust or make individual cookies. Or store leftovers in a dough ball, wrapped in plastic wrap, in the freezer for up to 12 months.
- You also can bake the crust up to 2 days in advance and add toppings right before serving.
- See page 166 for dairy-free chocolate chip suggestions.

Storage
- Keep leftover completed fruit pizza in an airtight container in the fridge for up to 2 days.

Resources and References

International readers: You can buy many of the gluten-free and allergy-friendly brands listed below from Amazon or Vitacost.

Baking/Cooking

Bob's Red Mill Dedicated Gluten-Free Products—gluten-free oats, quick oats, flaxseed/meal, chia seed, hemp seed, gluten-free all-purpose flour, chickpea flour, coconut flour, raw sugar, coconut sugar, unsweetened coconut flakes, chickpea flour

Other Gluten-Free Flour Mixes—Cup4Cup, King Arthur

Raw Sugars/Sugar Substitutes—Lakanto Classic Monk Fruit, Wholesome, Sugar in the Raw

Allergy-Friendly Chocolate/Baking—Enjoy Life Foods, Sunspire, Vitacost

Dye-Free Food Color and Sprinkles—Watkins, McCormick's Natural

Dairy-Free/Soy-Free Butter—Nutiva Plant-Based Ghee, Miyoko's Creamery

Dairy-Free/Soy-Free Cheese and Cheese Sauces—Violife, Daiya

Snacks/Bread

Gluten-Free Cereal/Puffed Cereal/Gluten-Free Granola—Arrowhead Mills, Nature's Path, Bob's Red Mill

Gluten-Free Cookies/Sweets—Glutino, Enjoy Life Foods, Schär (international)

Grain-Free and Gluten-Free Tortillas—Maria and Ricardo's, Siete, Food for Life Sprouted Corn Tortillas

Gluten-Free Chips—Siete, Kettle (avocado oil), Food Should Taste Good, Late July

International Gluten-Free Snacks/Bread—Schär

Condiments/Sauces

Gluten-Free Seasoning Mixes—Siete, Simply Organic Seasoning

Gluten-Free Condiments/Dips—Primal Kitchen, Chosen Foods

Gluten-Free/Soy-Free Worcestershire Sauce—Lea & Perrins The Original Worcestershire Sauce

Coconut Aminos—Coconut Secret, Bragg, Big Tree Farms

Pasta/Noodles

Gluten-Free Pasta—DeLallo, Banza, Jovial

Asian Noodles and Gluten-Free/Soy-Free Sauces—Thai Kitchen, San-J, Coconut Secret, Lotus Foods

Uncured/Nitrate-Free Deli

Applegate Farms—Uncured deli meat, bacon, turkey bacon, pepperoni

Heck (UK base) and Hatifield (US base)—Gluten-free sausage, chicken sausage, pork bacon

Supplements

Collagen Peptides/Gelatin—Further Food, Primal Kitchen, Vital Protein

Plant-Based Protein—Vega, Orgain, Garden of Life, Huel

About the Author

LINDSAY COTTER is a nutrition specialist for sports nutrition and gluten-free eating. In addition to being AASDN certified, she's the CEO and founder of the gluten-free recipes blog Cotter Crunch, and an oversharer with a passion for helping others thrive while enjoying good food, despite having food allergies. A trusted resource for all things gluten-free and allergy-friendly, she's been featured in Dr. Axe, *Shape* magazine, *Fitness* magazine, *Men's Health*, and more.

Today, she lives in Draper, Utah, with her husband and their Vizsla. In this book, you'll find Lindsay's love of food expressed through family-friendly versions of classic childhood dishes that have all the flavor you remember, are simple to make, and will have the whole family eager to gather around the dinner table.

Acknowledgments and Appreciation

This book would not have been published without the help of my devoted husband, parents, and amazing team (and dear friends) Shyanne Gregg, Ana Ankeny, Elle Queen, and Sammi Ricke.

To my husband, James, without you, Cotter Crunch would not exist. You are my muse and my main man, my rock! Thank you for taste-testing every last recipe and staying VERY late at the studio to help me cook and clean.

To my parents, thank you for your undying love and support. You believed in me and cheered me (us) on throughout this whole process. Thank you, Mom, for going through EVERY recipe with me, testing, testing, testing, writing, and rewriting again to ensure they're perfect. Also, for spending literally months away from home to help me. Thank you, Dad, for your generosity, for your entrepreneurship advice, and for going above and beyond to help make this cookbook mission possible!!

To my team (our team):

Shyanne Gregg, the woman who can literally read my brain (most of the time) and assemble the jumbled chaos into words. Shyanne, thank you for being an amazing editorial manager, recipe tester, and dear friend/sister. You brought this book to fruition with your writing and words! I am honored to be part of your life and to have you be part of mine, in business and all! Thank you for taking risks and making big changes to help bring our goals and vision to life!

To Ana Ankeny, my project manager and dear friend. I'm pretty sure I'd still be editing this book without you! What can I say? You are a godsend and always keep me on track! Thank you for your infectious optimistic attitude and dedication. Thank you for emergency flights to SLC, late nights on Marco, and lots of recipe testing. Thank you for checking EVERY SINGLE RECIPE not once but twice, and making sure they made sense and were easy to understand. Your involvement has been invaluable to this community and our team.

Thank you to Sammi Ricke (our main recipe tester) for testing MANY MANY recipes and for being our main cheerleader. Your positive attitude and encouragement kept us going. Thank you for believing in this book, for providing feedback, and for prayers.

I would also like to recognize Elle Queen and Myriam Desrosiers for helping test many recipes with your families, not only in this book but for Cotter Crunch as well!

And thank you, the reader, for picking up this book and taking part in gluten-free and allergy-friendly living. You got this!! We got this!

If interested, you can find more wholesome and delicious gluten-free recipes in my previous cookbook, *Superfood Nourishing Bowls*, and on my gluten-free/allergy-friendly recipe website, www.cottercrunch.com.

Index